Staying Pure in a Sex-charged World

Staying Pure in a Sex-charged World

Colin Dye
with
Amanda Dye

New Wine Press

New Wine Ministries
PO Box 17
Chichester
West Sussex
United Kingdom
PO20 6YB

ISBN 1-903725-46-1

Typeset by CRB Associates, Reepham, Norfolk
Cover design by CCD, www.ccdgroup.co.uk
Printed in the United States of America

Contents

Preface

The motivation for writing this book arose when I decided to deliver a teaching series on the subject of sexuality to the congregation at Kensington Temple. The purpose of the series was to address the real questions that Christians today are asking about how to handle their sexuality – especially in a world that is constantly bombarding them with images of a sexual nature and often promotes promiscuity with little conscience or responsibility.

In order to find out the real issues that people were struggling with, or simply confused about, we conducted a survey of our own congregation and asked them to submit any questions they had. My wife Amanda and I were in Brazil when we prayed about and agreed the topics that should be covered, based on the questions that were being submitted. Some of the ground we subsequently covered was surprising to me; surprising to the extent that, in an age of so called sexual liberation, there is still so much that the world has to discover about God's gift of sex.

Whether you are single or married, I trust that the material contained in this book will help you to better understand God's plan for human sexuality, and will bring you a new freedom as you come to understand your own sexuality in the light of God's Word.

Throughout the book I have tried to speak from the point of view of both men and women and so am grateful to Amanda for her contribution throughout the book and especially the chapters on *Walking in Sexual and Emotional Freedom* and *Freedom From Soul Ties* which assist in maintaining this balance.

Colin Dye
July 2005

CHAPTER 1

THE REAL JOY OF SEX

"Therefore a man shall leave his father and mother and be joined to his wife and they shall become one flesh. And they were both naked, the man and his wife, and were not ashamed."

(GENESIS 2:24–25)

Reading the Bible we find that God is very explicit and direct about the subject of sex and human sexuality. He knows everything there is to know about it – a fact that often escapes people's attention. God made the human body and there isn't anything that will shock Him or surprise Him about what He has made. Human sexuality is a gift from God, a wonderful, precious, pure and holy thing that is to be received from Him and used as a means of glorifying Him in the context of marriage. Rather than existing for our own gratification, our sexuality is really intended to be a blessing to our covenantal partner in marriage.

It is precisely because people's view of sex and sexuality has become so distorted, twisted, and has moved so far away from God's original intentions that I felt the need to write this book. My hope is that it will help us to come back to a balanced understanding of the truth about sex as revealed in the Scriptures. This chapter is about discovering the real source and purpose of our sexuality and the "real" joy of sex.

Some time ago, my wife Amanda and I brought a series of teaching to our church on the topic of sexuality, which now makes up the content of this book. We carefully prepared the topics we were to speak on and then set about presenting them to the church family. When I finally came to deliver the teaching contained in this chapter, the title surprised me: discovering the *real* joy of sex! What surprised me was not that sex could be a real joy, but that in the twenty-first century, after decades of the "sexual revolution", I could stand up and say that there is something the world has yet to discover about sex! It seems an astonishing claim, because sex is now one of the most talked about subjects in society. In one form or another, through innuendo, TV, radio, billboard advertisements, movies, chat show discussions, magazines and so on, sex is one of the most prominent topics on people's agendas.

The Age of Sexual Liberation

The 1960s brought about the liberalization of sexuality. We called it the sexual revolution. It was an era where contraception was freely and easily available, and experimentation and promiscuity was positively encouraged. This set the scene for the increasingly liberal attitudes we see in society today, and has meant that people tend to feel much "freer" about their sexuality. The sexual revolution also paved the way for the lifting of censorship restrictions at a number of levels. Sex education in schools is but one example.

But what has all this sexual "liberation" and so-called "freedom" meant in practice? In the twenty-first century we are now reaping the fruits of that of our past carelessness. The institution of marriage itself is under threat; the "normal" family unit is under threat; it is common for people to indulge in "alternative" lifestyles. There have also been rapid rises in teenage pregnancies, divorce rate, single parent families, and the appearance of the AIDS virus.

However, it is not the purpose of this book to become my vehicle for ranting and raving about the ills of society. My intention here is to take a positive look at human sexuality and to endeavour to help us regain a true biblical view of God's wonderful gift. Suffice to say this: the sexual revolution did not bring the *utopia* that people expected it would. We have discovered as a society that physical sexual satisfaction is *not enough* to bring happiness and fulfilment, and that we have been looking for answers in the wrong places. In all that has transpired in the last forty years, the *real* joy of sex has not yet been discovered.

THE "REAL" JOY OF SEX

In 1972 a now famous book by Dr Alex Comfort was published. It was called *The Joy of Sex*[1] and was essentially a "how to" sex manual. I personally have not read that book and am not recommending it! But I do know that it was heavy on illustrations and majored on the use of different sexual positions and techniques, as if the *joy* of sex was certainly and only found in the pursuit of the *physical pleasure* that it brings.

In lovemaking, of course there are skills to be learnt. One question that crops up constantly in the context of counselling is, "Is it right to experiment with different sexual positions?" The answer to this question must be "Yes", since God is a wonderful creative God who celebrates the diversity of His creation. Just because people have historically often referred to the "missionary position", it doesn't mean to say that is the only one that God has ordained!

Many Christians are unsure of exactly what is and isn't permissible in the bedroom. But such an attitude really misses the point. The principle of love must always govern and rule over all. Therefore, married couples can do anything they want together in the privacy of their own bedroom *as long* as it respects the other person in love, doesn't go against their wishes, and doesn't harm them in any way.

The most important thing to remember is that your sexuality is *not* God's gift to you. Your sexuality is God's gift to *your partner*, through you. In sex as in everything, it is more blessed to give than to receive. Your sexuality is to meet the needs of your marriage partner, because love first considers the other person. So provided both people are comfortable and at ease with it, there really are no rules that God lays down for sex.

That's amazing if you think about it, because it runs completely contrary to the reputation of "churchy", inhibited, religious, stuffy teaching that the Church is famous for in the eyes of many.

The Source of Our Sexuality

So where does the real joy of sex lie? It is in the discovery of its true source and purpose. You cannot understand or enjoy anything to the full unless you understand its origin and purpose. This is the most wonderful, positive, affirming thing about God's gift of sexuality – that it is simply that: a *precious gift.* In other words, God is the originator, the inventor and the creator of sex; sex was God's idea.

Genesis 1:27–28 says:

> *"So God created man in His own image; in the image of God He created him; male and female He created them. Then God blessed them, and God said to them, 'Be fruitful and multiply; fill the earth and subdue it; have dominion over the fish of the sea, over the birds of the air, and over every living thing that moves on the earth.' "*

The word "man" here, doesn't mean "male" as opposed to "female"; it means "humanity" – the generic word for the human race. The verse goes on to say that from the very beginning there was a single genus – one kind – but two *types* of human being: male and female.

It is obvious to anyone that there is a big difference between men and women – and that the difference is not merely biological or physical. But even if that was all the evidence we had, it is easy to establish the fact that the biological/physical makeup of men and women is different, yet complementary. Each has an inherent sexuality and that sexuality differs; each has different sexual organs that are made to fit together in a way that God our heavenly Father designed.

After God had created the first man and woman, the Bible says that "He blessed them" (Genesis 1:28). They were completely naked and unashamed before God at this point, and amazingly God's first command to them was to have sex! If that astounds you, go back and read the Scriptures again. God blessed Adam and Eve and immediately commanded them to be *fruitful* together and to *multiply* – i.e. to begin to reproduce. How could they do that without being intimately involved together? This revelation should blow our minds because, despite the fact that we have had decades of so-called sexual freedom in society, still people think that God is somehow against sex!

Some people have tried to suggest that the actual "act" of sex between Adam and Eve did not take place until after the Fall, and that this indicates sex is a "sinful" activity. But that cannot be the case since God clearly blessed Adam and Eve's sexuality, giving them the command to be fruitful and multiply, *before* the Fall. Scripture is not explicit about whether Adam and Eve "knew" each other before the Fall, but I would like to assume that they did. What reason did they have to wait? The Bible *is* explicit in recording that after the Fall Adam knew his wife and then they produced their first child. But in all probability they enjoyed a wonderful, harmonious, sexual relationship prior to this. Since I am arguing from silence, I won't try to press this point further.

The Purpose of Sex

The purpose of sex is blessing, intimacy, joy, pleasure, and multiplication. The Bible tells us that everything God created in the world was "good". Despite that, people still argue that sex is merely a means by which the multiplication God commanded is achieved, and that the Bible says nothing about *enjoying* the process. "Sex is a necessary evil, so you have to put up with it occasionally" has been the view of some – perhaps those who have overreacted to the promiscuity of modern society. But to think that the *only* purpose of sex is to produce children is to really misunderstand what the Bible teaches.

Much of the Christian Church has taught this for centuries, but this view takes sex right out of context. This is essentially what the world does in another way – it separates sex from its context of a loving, committed, marriage covenant. The Church has been at fault in teaching that sex is solely for procreation, which the Bible never teaches. This teaching in Church tradition goes back to the early Church fathers, some of whom castrated themselves in order to make sure that they didn't become unholy. They believed that sex was sinful, or at best sensual and fleshly.

There was even a teaching in the Church that the Holy Spirit left the bedroom when a married couple were having sex and only returned safely when it was all over! Others still teach today that celibacy is the highest standard of holiness. Personally, I do not understand how people can read that into the book of Genesis when God clearly instructed, "Go and be fruitful, fill the earth." Can anyone seriously contend that there is a better way of doing that by avoiding sex? I think they have misunderstood God's intentions.[2]

The Roman Catholic Church taught that marriage was a *sacrament*, a view also adopted by the Anglican Church at a certain point. This *sounds* good initially, because of the inference that marriage is *sacred* – and of course it is a sacred institution. But I have a feeling that the motivation behind such teaching was not so much to protect the sanctity of marriage, but to try to shield Christian marriage from the common sensual, pleasurable approach to human relationships that was prevalent in society at the time. Such teaching tried to suggest that marriage was such a holy thing that the physical aspect of it was irrelevant, other than for producing children.

A further teaching in Roman Catholicism seeks to perpetuate the idea of sex being fleshly and intolerable, which I believe is quite erroneous. There is a teaching which puts forward the idea that Mary, Jesus' mother, maintained her virginity throughout her life. When Roman Catholics talk about the virgin Mary, they don't simply mean that she was a virgin when she conceived Jesus, but that she never conceived afterwards and never had sex at all, remaining perpetually a virgin (the implication of which must be that somehow her hymen was miraculously preserved during childbirth). I understand Catholic doctrine wanting to so protect Mary, because she was an amazing and wonderful woman, but such teaching has done a great disservice to people's understanding of holiness and motherhood.

A Negative View of Sex

Years ago, as a church staff looking to better equip ourselves for praying and counselling others, we had a professional sex therapist come and speak to us. This lady was not a Christian, but she did teach us a lot of things. For instance, we were amazed when she told us that in her work she often came across women who had a number of children, but who totally denied that they had ever had sex! She used to say to them, "Well how did you have those babies?" to which they would typically respond, "Well my husband did something to me, but we never had sex." It astonished me that people will even deny the *existence* of sex because they have a negative view of it.

Similarly, it might surprise you to learn that in counselling situations, one of the major issues we regularly face is the non-consummation of Christian marriages. To me it seems amazing that people could be married for many years and yet never enjoy anything like a regular sex life, or possibly never have sex at all.

As Christian counsellors examining this phenomenon, there seemed to be two major reasons, both of which we can learn from.

Firstly (and understandably given the historical teaching of the Church), some Christians have been brought up with such a negative view of sex that they find themselves totally unprepared for any form of sexual relationship. They have either been so protected or so preconditioned that when they enter into marriage they are afraid, thinking that there is something wrong with sex and find it impossible.

Secondly, and perhaps more surprisingly, people who were far from sheltered, and who led a full sexual life before they came to Christ, often experienced problems after conversion. Because all their sexual experiences occurred outside of Christ and outside God's rules, they arrived at the incorrect conclusion that their sexuality was wrong. So when they subsequently married, they "shut down" sexually, because they associated *sex* with *sin*. Of course this is a wrong conclusion. Each person's sexuality is a gift from God. It's how you use it that makes the difference.

In summary, the real joy of sex has been crushed and trampled either by the rampant sexual immorality of society, or by the repressed attitudes and teaching of the Church. As a result we must rediscover the *real* and *true* joy of sex as God intended.

We know that God gave us sex for reproduction. That is made very clear from Scripture. But God also gave us sex for *enjoyment*. However, He gave it for our enjoyment according to specific criteria – and the most important criterion to God is that of *relationship*.

Made for Relationship

God made us to be relational beings, not just functional beings. We are not merely "animals" of a higher order than the rest. The so-called theory of evolution, which contains far more philosophical prejudice than hard science, says humanity is just another, more sophisticated, highly evolved branch of the animal kingdom. We are much more than this, we are relational beings, and we conduct our relationships in a way that is totally different from animals – in a way that reflects the nature of God Himself, in that we operate in a "covenantal" way that involves at least three things:

1. ***Social interrelationship***. We are social beings who need to interrelate. Just as God is not merely one person, He is also three – a trinity consisting of Father, Son and Holy Spirit – so we need to have a social communion. God made us to exist in groups, and the principal kind of grouping He has given us is that of marriage involving one male and one female. This leads on to:
2. ***Intimacy***. God designed us for intimacy in our relationships, just as there is intimacy in the Godhead – such a closeness that it makes it hard to know where one person ends and the other begins.
3. ***Unity***. The three distinct persons of the Godhead are also seen as one inseparable person and so it is in marriage as the two are seen as "one flesh" which means "one person". Just as the Godhead is one in essence and purpose, so when husbands and wives come together in relationship, they should be one in essence and purpose. That's God's agenda for marriage.

Unity is clearly very important to God and the fact that He sees a married couple as "one person" underlines this. One plus one equals one by God's reckoning. He expects that through marriage couples will develop unity of heart, purpose, and direction. That doesn't mean that we have to believe exactly the same things or say exactly the same things – there can be diversity within that unity – because that is what marriage is all about. God brings two very different people together and it makes for an interesting development of unity. But at the heart of all this is physical and sexual unity.

The difficulty about our modern society is that it nearly always attempts to reverse the proper biblical order for doing things. People invariably put sex first and then try to make the other factors in their relationship fit into place around it. God's focus however is first and foremost the establishment of a covenantal relationship. Once this is in place it brings unity and intimacy, and this is the perfect foundation on which to build a sexual relationship. This new physical dimension then serves to further deepen the unity and intimacy that has already been created. God didn't just give us sex in order to procreate, but to enhance our relationship also. If it was simply a means of reproduction, then God did not have to make it such a loving, beautiful, pleasurable, intimate act. He could have made it much easier than that. But God wanted to give us a special gift of love, joy, and pleasure that would be the holy of holies of the marriage relationship.

Sometimes I hear people voicing such questions as, "Is contraception wrong?" If they truly understood that sexuality in their marriage centred around *relationship*, then they would already know the answer to that question. If relationship, unity and intimacy are paramount, then you cannot conclude that every time you have sex it must be in order to produce children. Sex is there to cement your relationship. So, in order to be a responsible parent, I don't see any alternative to family planning through the use of contraception.[3]

Marriage then, is about developing deep unity between man and woman at every level: mind, emotions, vision, direction, spiritual, physical and sexual – and that is described by God in a wonderful, masterful way – really an understatement – yet full of revelation, when He says, the man and the woman were "naked" and "unashamed". That's God way of saying "Hey guys, I've got a wedding present for you. My wedding gift for you is sexual intimacy."

Sexuality and Marriage

Many single people are confused by certain passages in 1 Corinthians that seem to go against everything I've written about so far, so it would be useful to devote some space to examining them to find out what the apostle Paul was conveying to us.

1 Corinthians chapter 7 is a central passage that contains a number of interesting statements. Here we read such comments as, "It is better not to marry … if you are unmarried you will only be concerned about the Lord, but if you are married it will distract you from Him … only get married if you can't help yourself, because it is better to marry than to burn".

Have these verses ever puzzled you? It seems as though Paul is advocating singleness as the highest form of godliness.

First, it is important to note that Paul was not setting out a rule for all Christians of all times. He was primarily talking to the Christians in Corinth who were under a certain kind of distress, or persecution at that time. Paul refers to it when he makes remarks like, "in times like this . . ." and "in the current situation" which preface many of his thoughts. In other words he is saying, "Because of the persecution that is around at the moment, if you stay single you will save yourself a lot of hassle." Even so, he goes on to balance his statement with words to the effect of, "Having said that, even under those circumstances, if you do marry, you have not sinned."

Some people have the idea that Paul was against marriage, but actually Paul affirmed marriage very strongly. Why did he need to do this? Because in Paul's day, as today, there were religious people around who thought they were more spiritual than God! At the time such people were spreading false teachings about the nature of marriage, sexuality, the human body etc. Corinth was a melting pot of ideas and philosophical theories from a mix of cultures, and the Corinthian mindset was very much at work amongst the believers who lived there.

For instance, people were saying things such as, "Even though you are a Christian, because your husband/wife is not, you must not let them touch you sexually, because it could give their demons access to you!" In other words, they were convinced that a believer could be defiled by having a physical relationship with their unbelieving partner. However, Paul said, "If you are given to Christ, your holiness will deal with that." Paul countered such teaching by pointing out that, contrary to their argument, a Christian's faith actually *sanctified* their unbelieving partner. Paul was essentially saying, "Don't you realise that 'Greater is He that is in you, than he that is in the world'?" You have nothing to fear if you are married to a non-believer. You could be married to someone who is not in anyway godly, righteous or holy, yet your faith will influence them, and their ungodliness will not affect you. Paul, in fact, goes a step further and reminds us that it is *our responsibility* to love our husband or wife no matter what the circumstances, though we should not seek to marry unbelievers and thereby create an "unequal yoke".

At the beginning of 1 Corinthians 7 Paul sets out two important principles that encapsulate the way in which our sexuality within marriage should be handled. He makes it plain that:

1. Your sexuality is a gift for your partner in marriage.
2. He wants you to be a blessing to your husband/wife.

In 1 Corinthians 7:3, Paul says *"Let the husband render to his wife the affection due her, likewise also the wife to her husband."* Other translations are a little more explicit than that, but Paul is definitely talking about sex. He continues in verse 4, *"The wife does not have authority over her own body, but the husband does. Likewise, the husband does not have authority over his own body, but the wife does."* Paul is outlining God's desire for there to be total equality in the sexual relationship. This is something that has only really been rediscovered by society at large during the mid-twentieth century! And yet it was God's idea all along!

It was always God's plan that sexual relationships would be *completely mutual.* God gives you your sexuality on trust in preparation for you to give it to your spouse. Men, God gave your sexuality to you solely for your partner in marriage. That's why you have no business giving it to anybody else. And the same goes for women. Later on we'll see why that is so important. It's not just about laying down rules and regulations. There is something beautiful and precious about sexuality which has been all but destroyed in our modern generation, and which we as Christians must recover and rediscover. Imagine a relationship in which the husband is so committed to the joyful, intimate, sexual fulfilment of his wife that he dare not enter the marriage bed with any other motive than being a blessing to her. And at the same time, his wife is one hundred percent committed to his sexual and emotional fulfilment. This is truly fulfilling God's biblical mandate for marital relations and the world has yet to see the power of that.

1 Corinthians 7:5 is a real shocker to some people. Paul says to married people regarding sex, *"Do not deprive one another."* What does this mean? Exactly what it says! But why did God need to command people to have regular sex? Again I believe that Paul is speaking to the Corinthian mindset (and to our modern-day mindset too, because we are thoroughly influenced by the same Greek way of thinking). In Greek thought there was a clear division between the sacred and the secular. The body was thought of as belonging to that which was secular, earthly and base, as opposed to spiritual, holy and sanctified. The Corinthian Christians had got the idea that, having been saved, they were "too holy" to have sex and indulge in such activities of the flesh. Imagine, a woman getting saved and joining the local church in Corinth. Perhaps she would come home and tell her husband, "I have just been saved, that's the good news ... the bad news is, no sex." "But you're my wife!" the

husband would protest. "Never mind that, I am too holy for that stuff now." Paul was dealing with such false spirituality in this passage.

I don't want anyone reading this to come under condemnation about the way in which they conduct their relationship with their spouse, but I would go so far as to say that if you are *not* thinking about the fulfilment of your partner's needs in marriage, then something is wrong. Simply, if you only ever put your own needs first, then you are not fully honouring God.

Continuing with the rest of Paul's statement, we read:

> *"Do not deprive one another except with consent for a time, that you may give yourselves to fasting and prayer; and come together again so that Satan does not tempt you because of your lack of self-control."*
>
> (1 Corinthians 7:5)

Paul points out that there will be special times when as a couple you may need to have a time of concentrated, focused prayer and fasting – perhaps to see a specific breakthrough in prayer. Fasting is all about denying your normal drives and desires for a time in order to seek God more intensely – hence it makes sense to abstain from sexual relations for a time. But God understands well that the sexual drive He has given us is an extremely potent force, and so He specifies that it must be only "for a time" and then the couple are to resume normal relations.

The strength of our sexual drive is something that the enemy can easily capitalise on – which is why we should protect our sexuality so diligently. It is the reason why sex or sensuality is used constantly by the media to sell us everything from soap to shoes to cars. It works because the sexual content attracts our attention very easily. But there is nothing worse than seeing God's precious, personal, intimate gift being paraded in such a degrading way on billboards, magazines and television. Our sexuality has such dynamic potential that God insists we keep it safe within the heart of marriage.

The word "sex" has found its way into popular idiom and is now deeply ingrained, but the Bible uses a much more beautiful and subtle description, which is the phrase "to know". We read that Adam "knew" his wife and so forth. This is a wonderful way of speaking about the physical aspect of marriage. The world has sought to reduce this act merely to "having sex" – a purely functional and selfish act – whereas God's emphasis is upon an act that is not just functional but relational: the husband and wife have "knowledge" of each other. In fact, God's ideal is that they literally know *all there is to know* about each other over time. "Knowing" speaks of an ongoing covenant in which you are committed to your marriage partner in every dimension of life.

Preserving Your Sexuality

It is precisely because of the potency of sexuality in the context of marriage that the devil works so hard to get people to "give away" their sexuality outside of that covenant relationship. The hedonistic culture of modern society makes it ever more difficult for people, especially young people, to save themselves for their future marriage partner.

To young people today I always say, "draw a line". It is important to recognise your limits and not go beyond them. Don't play near the edge of the precipice in your relationships with others. Safeguard God's very precious gift to you of your sexuality for the one person you will be committed to in marriage. Your virginity will be your ultimate wedding gift to your husband or wife. If it's already too late for that, don't despair. God can bless you, forgive you and restore you. All of that and more is not beyond Him and the cleansing power of the blood of Christ. But remember that intimacy is fragile and it needs security. The security needed to protect it is the marriage relationship. You should never give yourself to a person who has no intention of ultimately being in a covenant relationship with you.

Chapter Summary

- The Bible is explicit and direct about the subject of sex and human sexuality. Sex is a gift from God that is not intended for our own gratification, but for our future marriage partner.
- The joy of sex is not found simply in the physical act, but in being a blessing to your marriage partner.
- God is not against sex as some sections of the Church have taught or inferred historically. He created it; it was His idea and His gift. His first command to Adam and Eve was to engage in a fulfilling sexual relationship and to bear fruit.
- The purpose of sex is blessing, intimacy, joy, pleasure, and multiplication. God did not give us the gift of sexuality so that we could reproduce only.
- God made us relational beings, just as He is relational. His desire for us is unity and intimacy in the context of marriage. This becomes the foundation for a fulfilling sexual relationship, which in turn further cements unity and intimacy.
- In 1 Corinthians 7 the apostle Paul confirms two important principles regarding the physical aspect of marriage: (1) your sexuality is a gift for your partner in marriage, and (2) He wants you to be a blessing to your husband/wife.
- Our sexual drive is extremely potent and for that reason it must be guarded with care. It is because it is so strong that God commands it to be protected within the security of the marriage relationship.
- Even if you have made mistakes and feel that you have let God down through sexual sin, He can restore you and the blood of Jesus can cleanse you completely. If this is true for you, seek God and talk to Him about it. If necessary, approach a trusted friend/church leader to pray through the issue with you.

GOD'S WAY AND OUR WAY

In June 2004, a UK weekend newspaper, *The Independent on Sunday*, ran a feature entitled, "No Sex, Please: We're (British) Teenagers. It's a Silver Ring Thing." The "silver ring thing" phenomena has swept America and now has found its way to the UK, but it has largely been ridiculed by the media, although some politicians have spoken in favour of it. The movement is about young people making the decision to remain virgins until they are married. It doesn't come exclusively from a Christian perspective, but is about young people wanting to stand out from the crowd and live unashamedly pure lives.

In the newspaper feature, two girls and one guy – all seventeen years old – were interviewed about their vows of celibacy until marriage. One girl, Alex, said, "I have seen my friends and their relationships and many do have serious regrets. There's no closeness to their relationships – that's not shown in the media." The young man, David, said, "When I marry, I won't be comparing one person with two or three others before. You get the chance to learn a lot about the other person without all the added pressure of sex." The last girl declared, "My mum bought me a ring two years ago and I promised to wear it until I'm married. It's my decision too. It's the only way you can live without the risk of STDs (sexually transmitted diseases) and pregnancy."

So why does the media scoff at such an initiative where teenagers are expressing a desire to keep their bodies pure for their marriage partner? Is it sheer scepticism or simply disbelief? Nevertheless, this is what one high profile British politician had to say about it:

> "The silver ring thing is coming to Britain, doubtless to a chorus of mockery from our libertarian media and commentators who resolutely refuse to see that the 'do anything you like' experiment of the last few decades has been a disastrous failure and at tremendous human cost.
>
> Britain has the highest teenage pregnancy rate in western Europe. Behind that bold statistic is the reality of unplanned and ill-prepared motherhood, stolen youth, fatherless children, poverty and hopelessness. In hard-pressed health services Britain devotes scare resources and millions of pounds to the prevention

and cure of HIV Aids, to clinics specialising in venereal disease and to the killing of the unborn and unwanted. Even if there were no moral issues involved, the economic cost of sexual licence and the suffering that follows in its wake should give us pause for a great deal of thought.

We are told, farcically, that the answer is more sex education and greater availability of contraception. The facts scream otherwise. We have never had so much sex education and never so much contraception and the result is a vast increase in teenage pregnancy. There is a foolproof way to prevent an unwanted pregnancy: don't do the thing that produces babies. There is a foolproof way to avoid the spread of HIV Aids: have sex only with one faithful partner. Yet the health and educational establishments refuse to treat abstinence as a serious option.

Uganda once had the highest rate of HIV Aids in the world, but in the past decade the disease has dropped from striking 30% of the population to 10%. Experts attribute this dramatic success to a 'true love waits' campaign, in which schools and religious organisations have promoted abstinence before marriage. In the US the campaign is regarded as sufficiently successful in combating teenage pregnancy to have attracted generous funding from the government. Great Britain, take note! Libertarian methods have failed. Let those who have promoted them as infallible for so long, now shut up and give the silver ring thing a fair hearing among the young."

(Anne Widdicombe, Conservative MP)

It is good when people observe that moral principles are valuable because they make good common sense, not simply on the grounds of religious dogma. It is gratifying when people see that God's ways are best; when they acknowledge that God knows what He is doing. It is true that when we follow His guidelines, that obedience brings the greatest amount of blessing into our lives.

As the MP stated, there are very good moral, spiritual, practical, economic and social reasons why God has given us His rule book. It is after all, the Maker's Manual. And yet, apart from a few oases of hope such as the silver ring thing movement, it seems that the majority are determined to go their own way and exalt so-called "freedom of choice" over consequence. Not only that, but promiscuity is so rampant that many find themselves trapped in sexual addictions as powerful as drug addictions, unable to break free.

Going God's Way Is Truly Liberating

To some, "freedom from sexual bondage" might seem a strange combination of words. Most people in our post-modern society are crying freedom from rules and regulations. Surely freedom means that you can do what you want, doesn't it? Such people would no doubt regard God's rules for living as "bondage", and indeed biblical principles are often mocked by society. But I want to promote the truth that in fact, God's rules are liberating.

By way of illustration, picture this scene: a high speed train is hurtling along its tracks towards its destination. Now imagine the same train leaping off its tracks, crying freedom and running across open fields, completely out of control.

Which of these scenarios is a true picture of freedom? The train running smoothly along its tracks as it was designed to, or the train hurtling out of control, throwing passengers out, killing and destroying right across the field? If a train leaps its tracks, it's not free – it's dangerous.

To use another illustration, imagine you go out to a concert one evening to hear a solo pianist perform. You are expecting to hear some relaxing classical music or perhaps some jazz, but the pianist announces that he is a "free" musician and is going to play some of his own compositions. Being a "free" musician means that he doesn't believe in or follow any of the conventional rules of music – he just plays a random, discordant and unrelated series of notes and chords. How many of us could listen to that for any length of time? Maybe you would you like to go to such a concert – but that's just the novelty element!

The fact is, all good music is expressed within the framework of a set of rules which are interpreted in various creative ways. Even a genre such as jazz, which many consider to be very "free" in its expression, has certain rules that govern it. A jazz pianist will drop the root note of his chords and "colour" them by sharpening or flattening notes in the middle – to put it roughly! But he is still moving within predefined boundaries to express subtle nuances of sound.

In both these examples there are principles at work that, when followed, produce something orderly, beautiful and lovely. That is what I commend to you about God's ways for human sexuality. God's ways are truly liberating and as we abide by them, we are blessed. In Romans 12:1–2 the apostle Paul instructs us to surrender our bodies to God according to His will so we will "prove" that God's way is best:

> *"I beseech you therefore, brethren, by the mercies of God, that you present your bodies a living sacrifice, holy, acceptable to God, which is your reasonable service. And do not be conformed to this world, but be transformed by the renewing of your mind, that you may prove what is that good and acceptable and perfect will of God."*

This passage raises some important principles. First of all, God says, "I want you to present your bodies to me." In the twenty-first century we are more aware of our bodies than ever before. The mass media has actively promoted a "body awareness" that has often been taken to excess with the likes of plastic surgery and "extreme makeovers". But Paul insists that our bodies should be surrendered to God.

When Paul wrote these words, he was not thinking just of the physical body, but of bringing your whole being – body, soul (emotions, personality) and spirit – in surrender to God's purposes. But obeying God does have a lot to do with *physical* obedience.

Scripture has a lot to say about the body – it is given by God; made by God; endowed with a range of desires that need to be fed in order for it to function at an optimum level – including normal, healthy sexual desires. But God says, "Don't treat your bodies like the world treats theirs. Bring what I have given you back to Me and place it on My altar, because by so doing you will not be conformed to this world and you will be blessed."

Here lies one of the great difficulties that all Christians face and the reason why so many people, Christian or not, are trapped in sexual sin: instead of surrendering their bodies to God and letting them be governed by Him, they are taking their morality from what is happening around them in society. People are watching movies and television programmes and learning values which they believe are values to live by. Yet, God offers us alternative: to not be pressed into the world's mould of conformity, but to be transformed by the renewing of our minds.

So what is the renewing of your mind? In essence it is to understand that God's way is the way that brings liberty, freedom, joy, fullness and happiness. In this regard God goes further than simply saying, "Trust Me, it will work," He says, "If you obey Me, I'll prove to you that it works! I'll prove to you that My way is 'good and acceptable and perfect'."

The Story of Eden

If you go God's way, you will soon be able to prove that God's way is best. Why then, is it such hard work to convince people of that fact? One of the key reasons is that we are living on "the other side" of the Fall in the Garden of Eden, which we read about in Genesis chapter 3.

In this account of Adam and Eve's disobedience to God and subsequent downfall, we read that the enemy, Satan, appears in the form of a snake and deceives Eve. What he does is to present a false picture of God to Eve, suggesting that He is a party pooper. "God," the devil says, "wants to restrict you; He wants to make rules; He is a killjoy dictator; all He wants to do is make you miserable. He has given you so many rules to follow that if you had any sense you would rebel against them and do your own thing. Find your own path – that's the key to true joy and happiness."

This is the lie that has pervaded man's thinking since the Fall, and it is the lie that every person will believe who does not have a renewed mind. But it is a lie from the snake.

The reality is that God's way is best. He is the Creator, the Life-giver, and going God's way brings *life* and not death. It brings fulfilment. But it is only pleasing if you follow God's way out of your own choice. It is never pleasing, never fulfilling, if you are *forced* to do it. If you are forced to live this way, then it makes you miserable; but if you choose it from your heart, it liberates you. This is why God gave us the free will to choose.

Problems have been caused by "religious", albeit well-meaning people who have become oppressive in their insistence to force patterns of behaviour upon people that those people are unwilling to accept in their heart. Instead of beating people over the head with the guilt and shame of their lack of compliance to God's rules, we should be showing them the truth of how they could be liberated, gently bringing them to a place where their hearts long for that liberty. Remember the "silver ring thing" teenagers at the beginning of this chapter? If their parents had tried to force them into complying with those standards, they certainly would have rebelled. Instead they discovered for themselves that God's way is best and they are making the right choices.

Moral Freedom and its Responsibility

God has given us freedom of choice so that we can be morally free people and make our own choices. He has no desire for us to be like puppets in His control. But with freedom of choice comes responsibility. We make our choices and we carry the responsibility for those choices. This ability is what sets us apart as human beings; it is part of our God-given dignity and is an amazing privilege. God will give us the guidance we need to make the right choices, because He wants us to have all of the facts, but we are the ones who choose. The devil's tactic, just as he demonstrated with Eve, is to present us with a choice *without* giving us all the facts. Temptation does not give us all the facts; temptation gives us the impression that if we participate in whatever is appealing to us, then it will bring fulfilment.

The Bible is quick to acknowledge that there is pleasure in sin; it doesn't try to deny that. But it makes clear to us that the pleasure of sin is short term, fleeting, superficial, and once that pleasure has gone it leaves only bondage and loss of freedom in its place. Here is the equation: when we exercise our freedom away from God, we lose freedom and end up in bondage. But when we exercise our freedom in the favour of God's way, we find true liberation in our lives.

Sin is *always* the wrong choice. The Bible says that:

"There is a way that seems right to a man,
But its end is the way of death."

(Proverbs 14:12)

God had told Adam and Eve explicitly that if they ate fruit from the tree of the knowledge of good and evil, they would die. God knew that if sin entered the realm of man it would spoil everything and lead to death. It is sin that has spoiled God's gift of sex to mankind, just like sin spoils everything. The devil wanted to make sin look attractive and hide its true consequences, so he said, "You will surely not die," but of course they did, because at the moment when they sinned, death set in. Similarly, the world does everything it can to make sex look attractive, whilst shunning its consequences.

We used to sing an old chorus, many years ago: "For me to live is Christ, to die is gain. There is no peace, no joy, no thrill like walking in His will." As a young Christian this song helped me a lot. I discovered that to go God's way could be thrilling and bring peace, joy, and fulfilment. We must reject the lie of our society that says, "Do this and you'll have a good time." The fact is people are not having a good time – not ultimately.

The Facts About God's Way

Following God's way in regard to our sexuality will bring blessing to us as individuals and to society as a whole. There are three things about going God's way that are important for us to understand:

1. It is "God's way" and not church rules or religious tradition

Doing things "God's way" is not about following the rules of the church or adhering to longstanding church tradition. When you follow God's way, you are following the way of the Word of God, the Maker's instruction manual. There is a difference! One would hope that church life and all it entails would be perfectly in line with the Word of God, but unfortunately that is not always the case. Often we are overrun with people's opinions about sexuality and what it means, that are not necessarily biblical. That is why we need to bring the Word of God to bear on our church life, to continually reform it over and again, because human or "religious" thinking regularly takes control and leaves us with so many rules that life is lost altogether.

Neither is "going God's way" simply following whatever you have historically been taught that God says about sexuality. When you look at it in the Bible, it is liberating to find that God gave sex to mankind as a gift that brings fulfilment in marriage. It is not shameful, embarrassing, ugly or disgraceful as some have suggested. Neither was it created simply for the continued propagation of the human species. It was God's intention from the beginning that it should be enjoyed and produce fruit and multiplication. He was blessing us to go and enjoy sex within the boundaries of marriage!

2. God's way gives you the "why" and not just the "what"

God doesn't just tell us *what* we must do, but He explains *why* it will be good for us. In other words, God's way is not just a list of things you should and shouldn't do – God gives us an explanation because He treats us as mature people. When you are bringing up children, as soon as they can possibly understand (which is much sooner than you think), give them the "why" about the things you want them to do, not just the "what". We want them to understand *why* they must wash their hands and *why* they must brush their teeth – not because it makes mummy and daddy happy, or unhappy when they don't do it, but because it is valuable and necessary in and of itself. If you do that, then your children will begin to accept responsibility for their own lives. Similarly, God helps us to understand why certain restrictions are necessary and why He requires we obey them.

3. God's way is not just "rule-based", it shows you "how to"

God goes further than just *telling us* that His way is best, or even *explaining* why it is best for us. He shows us "how to" live according to His ways. And that is really the heart of the matter. God's way is not about pointing the finger at us and saying what is right and what is wrong to make us feel bad. It is about understanding and experiencing the power and beauty of this thing, human sexuality, under God's power. Therefore, God doesn't just give us rules and principles, but the Bible is very practical in its approach to guiding us – it shows us not only "what" and "why", but "how to".

Having acknowledged that God's way is the best way and that it will bring blessing and fulfilment into our lives, in the next chapter we will look at exactly what is sexual sin, why it is wrong, and the steps we need to take in order to break free from it.

Chapter Summary

- God's ways are best and biblical principles are common sense. When we follow God's guidelines, that act of obedience brings the greatest amount of blessing into our lives.
- God's rules for living are often mocked by society and thought of as restrictive, but actually they are liberating. God's principles, when followed, produce something orderly and beautiful.
- Our bodies were made by God and endowed with a range of drives that need to be fed for us to function properly – including normal, healthy sexual desires.
- The Bible teaches that we must surrender our bodies to God and let them be governed by Him. We must not take our moral values from society, but have our minds renewed according to God's values.
- God has given us freedom of choice so that we can be "morally free" people, but with freedom of choice comes responsibility. God will give us the guidance we need to make the right choices, because He wants us to have all of the facts, but we are the ones who choose.
- Doing things "God's way" is not about following the rules of the church or church tradition, it is about following the Word of God, the Maker's instruction manual.
- God doesn't just tell us *what* we must do, but He explains *why* it will be good for us.
- God does not just give us rules, He shows us *how* to live.

CHAPTER 3

WHAT IS SEXUAL SIN AND WHY IS IT WRONG?

To really understand sexual sin and why it is wrong and harmful requires us to understand our human sexuality and how it was created and designed to function by God. God's gift of sex to mankind was one part of His covenantal blessing to us and was created by Him to be the holy of holies of human relationships within the bounds of *marriage.*

That's how God designed it to be used. Any use of sex outside those boundaries is a perversion of God's design.

God made marriage to be a "covenant" between a man and a woman – that means a binding agreement. The marriage covenant is also intended to be a "public" covenant that is open and recognised before society. It's not an agreement that couples can make five minutes before having sex in an "I love you, you love me, so it's alright" kind of way! It is not informal, but highly serious.

Marriage ceremonies have taken place in many different shapes and forms throughout history. It hasn't always resulted in a little piece of paper which declares you legally married. But marriage has always been, from the beginning, an open declaration to society that this man and this woman are covenanting together.

The Sanctity of the Marriage Covenant

A covenantal agreement is very serious language in God's vocabulary. He describes His own relationship with us and our relationship with Him as a covenant. Because God has revealed Himself to us in covenant relationship, it indicates that He wants human relationships, especially marriage, to mirror our relationship with Him.

What kind of covenant is marriage? In both Proverbs 2:17 and Malachi 2:14 God describes marriage as a covenant of *companionship*. When you covenant with your husband or your wife in marriage, you are promising to be one another's companion for life. But this is no ordinary type of companionship. It is not like the companionship between a man and his dog; it is not even like the companionship between a man and his brother, or a father and his son. It is a form of companionship between a man and a woman that goes far beyond such relationships into a place of deep intimacy where two people become effectively "one person". Genesis 2:24 says that the two, "become one flesh" and are joined together inseparably. Sexual intimacy is the holy of holies of the expression of that companionship.

Of course, the marriage relationship is not all about sex, but it has sex at its centre, protected by everything else around it. It has parallels with the pattern that God used for the design of the Old Testament tabernacle, which is why I refer to sex as the holy of holies of marriage. The tabernacle was a tent-like cathedral, a house of worship that was prefabricated and could be carried around as the people of Israel travelled through the wilderness. There was an outer court, inner courts, an altar of sacrifice with a basin to wash in, and then there were two separate sections which were hidden from view. One was called "the holy place" and the other was called "the most holy place" or the "holy of holies". The holy of holies was the most special place of all.

God has given us this relationship of sex as the holy of holies of all our human relationships. When a husband and wife unite with one another in the act of sex, it is to be within the protection, covering and context of covenant, like the protective outer courts of the tabernacle. It is a sacred act which is not to be taken outside that protective covering. If it is taken outside and abused, then it is outside God's order and becomes a destructive force.

Why is it so destructive? Because as human beings we are made up of spirit, soul and body. When we present ourselves to the Lord as living sacrifices, as Paul instructs us to in Romans 12:1–2, we are giving the whole of ourselves to God, spirit, soul and body. Similarly, when we give ourselves to our husband/wife in the covenant of marriage, we are giving not just our body, but our soul and spirit too. In that act of union we are not accomplishing something merely in the physical realm, but in the spiritual as well.

That's why the act of sex is so serious. The Bible confirms the fact that we are "spirit, soul and body" people in 1 Thessalonians 5:23. When two people have sex, it is not just a physical act as the world would like us to believe. Those people are mixing their souls and merging their human spirits. It is not something to be taken lightly. God designed the act of intercourse to be a "seal" on the covenant of marriage, just as other types of covenant are sealed with blood.

In fact, the nature of the human body shows us that marriage too is a kind of blood covenant. God's intention is for a man and woman to both be virgins as they come to the marriage bed. As the husband penetrates his wife for the first time there is a separation or tearing of the woman's hymen which produces a small amount of blood. Even if the hymen is broken or not totally intact due to some activity other than sexual intercourse such as physical exercise, there is usually a small amount of blood produced by the first act of sexual intercourse. It is like a blood seal on the covenant of marriage and is an important reason why you should remain a virgin until then.

That's How God Made Us

The Bible says in 1 Corinthians 6:15–20 that when you "join" to another person through sex you become as one body with that person, *"For 'the two ... shall become one flesh'"* (verse 16). This passage goes on to say in verses 18–19:

> *"Flee sexual immorality. Every sin that a man does is outside the body, but he who commits sexual immorality sins against his own body. Or do you not know that your body is the temple of the Holy Spirit who is in you, whom you have from God, and you are not your own? For you were bought at a price; therefore glorify God in your body and in your spirit, which are God's."*

This is primarily what the world does not understand and what leads people to become trapped in sexual sin. If it was just about what you did with your body, that would be one issue. But the fact is, what you do with your body involves the whole of your being, and that leads to parts being ripped out of your soul as you fall in and out of illicit sexual relationships. If that is the case for you, then you need to be rescued from that and receive healing.

No wonder there are so many damaged people in our society. People fail to recognise the damage that they inflict on themselves and others as they plunder God's gift. Perhaps some reading this are feeling condemned because they have slept around in the past, or maybe you lost your virginity to someone other than your marriage partner? Thank God, there is good news. God can restore to you a purity of spirit and heart before Him, and He can wash all those sins away by the blood of another covenant: the blood of Jesus Christ, God's Son, that washes and cleanses every sin. You can be, in the eyes of God and in the eyes of your husband or wife, a "virgin", if you will allow God to bring that healing into your life. But God does not usually act to restore the physical effects of previous sexual sin – such as the rupture of the hymen. In that sense the loss of virginity is final and can never be restored. This shows the real value of virginity.

God is a Restorer and a Healer, but we must realise that all sin has consequences. Suppose you had committed murder before you became a Christian and you repented. Do you believe that God would forgive you and cleanse you with the blood of Jesus? Of course He would. But does it bring that dead man back to life? No. Similarly, there is a physical price to pay for sexual sin – a price that society has scorned and lied about for years, and still does when it mocks young people who choose to remain virgins until marriage. The whole of society, those trendy, sophisticated, artistic elitists, pour condemnation and ridicule upon any young person wanting to live a pure life. But I want to tell you, there's time to draw a line in the sand and say, "Let's help our young people understand and preserve the precious gift of virginity."

Having understood then, the framework within which sex is meant to function, and the seriousness of the act of sex in spiritual terms, how can we best define sexual sin? Simply put, it is any sexual thought or act which is not directed in love to the fulfilment of your partner in marriage. Wow! When we define it like that who amongst us could say we have not sinned?

It's very clear that we all need the mercy, forgiveness and grace of God in this area. One of the things I find obnoxious about many "religious" people is that they are so willing to condemn others when they sin or fall in this area – yet those same people who are heaping condemnation on others are, in the eyes of God, just as sinful.

We Have to Admit We Fall Short of God's Ideal

The Bible makes it clear that God has an ideal when it comes to human sexuality. But the Bible also says, *"all have sinned and fall short of the glory of God"* (Romans 3:23). With sex, as with all of life, we have to admit that in one way or another, in thought, word or deed, we have fallen short of God's standard. Even so, that need not breed guilt, despair and depression in us – rather it should drive us to our knees in prayer to approach our gracious God and say, "Lord please restore my broken sexuality."

We have seen that sex is to be preserved solely for marriage, but what is God's standard for our sexuality generally and how can we abide by it? There are four important areas we need to give our attention to if we are to exercise self-control over our sexuality and use it properly for the glory of God.

1. Our Love

The highest possible expression of your sexuality is love directed towards your marriage partner. If love is the driving force behind your sexuality it will prevent you from being selfish and taking advantage of your partner. Your sex drive should be directed in love to the fulfilment of your partner, because your sexuality is God's gift to him/her and not for self-gratification. This is why sex is aptly and rightly called "lovemaking". You give of yourself to your partner, and in giving you also receive. So love is the foundation and framework for sex.

2. Our Thoughts

Secondly, God's standard involves our thoughts. Jesus said in Matthew 5:27–30 that if you look lustfully upon a woman you've already committed adultery with her in your heart. In other words, our sexuality is a *heart issue* and we have to guard carefully what thoughts we allow ourselves to think, before they become embedded in our heart and eventually lead to sinful actions.

Essential to guarding your thought life and heart is policing what you allow to enter through your "eye gate". What do you allow your eyes to gaze upon and therefore dwell on in your mind? This is a critical area especially for men, who are easily aroused sexually by what they see. Jesus said, if your right eye offends you pluck it out! We wouldn't do that literally, but we do need to train ourselves to be careful what we look at.

The male eyes are like two red-hot heat-seeking devices scouring 360 degrees for any provocative image! They need to be held in check! In our men's group we often talk about "bouncing" your eyes – in other words, if your eyes see something that is not going to be helpful to you, you need to "bounce" your eyes straight off it and look at something else!

If only ladies knew – and I'm sure most do – how easily men were distracted by what they see, then they might have a little more compassion on their brothers in church by being more conscious of how they dress! The images that enter the eye gate and subsequently the mind affect the most powerful sexual organ in the body – the brain. But it is possible to train yourself to guard your eyes and your thoughts.

3. Our Emotions

If men are stimulated mostly by what they see, then women are mostly stimulated on an emotional level. A danger area for women is when they are feeling the need for security, love and companionship, and they begin to look for a member of the opposite sex who will meet that need. Be careful because your emotions can cause you to open right up and will make you vulnerable to a man who may have selfish motives and take advantage of you.

Here also is something that men need to learn – the power of touch. The apostle Paul said under certain circumstances it's good for a man not to touch a woman and he was speaking about the sexual relationship. Men often do not realise just what their physical proximity to a woman will do to her. It can awaken emotions in her that should not be awakened. Men, be very careful how you touch a woman, even in friendship, because women are made in a certain way and their emotions are very responsive to touch. It might just be gentleness on your part, with no sexual intent, but if only you knew what pain you were causing on the inside, you wouldn't do it.

4. Our Actions

Inevitably thoughts and emotions lead to actions, which is why it is so important to catch thoughts early and keep our hearts pure. I don't wish to dwell on the negative here, but many people have written to me asking questions about what sexual sin is, how it is defined, and what is acceptable and not acceptable for a believer. Some issues are obvious; others are not so obvious.

Adultery or fornication

Obvious sexual sins include adultery – a married person having sex with someone who is not their husband/wife; and fornication – promiscuous sex between unmarried people or simply "sex before marriage". Society tends to turn more of a blind eye towards fornication than it does to adultery. The world's mindset is, "We love each other, we respect each other and we're not hurting anyone, so it doesn't really matter." But for believers, it really does matter! If you truly love and respect one another, then remember the covenant!

Modern society has tried to erode the value of the marriage covenant. People live together in trial marriages because they want to make sure that, among other things, they are "sexually compatible". But in this business, you don't get to test drive! Do you know statistics show that people who live together in trial marriages are much more likely to divorce and separate? The Bristol Community Family Trust has recently warned that three-quarters of all family breakdowns affecting young children now involve unmarried parents. Their research shows that unmarried parents are five times more likely to break up than married parents.

Also, many women are pressured into sex before marriage by men who say, "I'm interested in you and I'm thinking maybe we'll get married so what's wrong with going to bed?" But the Bible says this is fornication.

Masturbation

One subject on which many people have questions is masturbation. It is a difficult area and I don't want to bring anybody reading this book under condemnation, but there are some principles to consider which should guide us as to whether masturbation is permissible or not.

A question that crops up time and again is, "Surely it is OK to give yourself some sexual relief occasionally?" I believe there is need for a lot of compassion and understanding here, especially for single people who have not emulated their peers, but have sought to keep themselves exclusively for their future partner in marriage. But there are three things that must be considered:

1. The context of sex is not self-enjoyment, but to bring pleasure to and bless your husband or wife. When you have sex with yourself (if you can describe it as such) it is so inwardly-focused that it becomes the very opposite of the purpose of sex.
2. The Bible speaks about self-control and not being mastered by anything. The difficulty with masturbation is that it often can end in *habitual* masturbation and bring a person into bondage. As a Christian pastor and counsellor I've seen down through the years what a terrible bondage this can be.

3. Finally, masturbation inevitably involves lust. I remember one pastor preaching and trying so hard to help people in this area. He was trying to be loving, but he said something so ridiculous: "Masturbation is OK as long as you don't think lustful thoughts and it doesn't become a habit." But lust and habitual bondage are the very things that masturbation tends to lead to!

Compared to the damage that such sins as adultery can cause, masturbation is, by all accounts, not the worst sin in the world. But the worst aspect of it is the guilt, condemnation and self-destruction that it produces. Guilt just complicates and worsens the problem of bondage, but thank God with the Holy Spirit's help it is possible to break out of this.

Other physical acts

Another area where people have difficulty drawing clear lines, especially courting couples, is what is permissible (ruling out intercourse) before marriage? There are other physical acts between people which, a little like playing too near the edge of a cliff, can cause them to eventually plummet into sexual sin. Initially it may fall short of fornication, but unchecked it will certainly end by going further than either person imagined it would.

The fact is, no one can stand in a pulpit and say, "When you go out with a boy or a girl you can do this, you can do that, but you can't do this, you can't do that." Nowhere in the Bible do we have such a set of rules. Each of us is made differently, so what is important is for you, if you are a single person, to understand what are your limits before you are brought into a place of temptation and sin against your own body and somebody else.

Clearly, any sort of genital acts constitute sexual sin; and kissing and touching in a way that stimulates your boyfriend or girlfriend to the point of distraction and utter temptation is, at the very least, stupid. The rule is: if you want to avoid doing something, you don't get as close as you can to it without actually doing it – you've got to set sensible boundaries according to your own limits.

Pornography

In modern society the proliferation of sexual images (used extensively for selling products in the media) and the free availability of pornography means that believers must be more vigilant than ever to guard their purity effectively. More and more homes have personal computers connected to the internet, and now high speed broadband is rapidly overtaking much slower dial-up connections – meaning of course, that images and streaming video can be viewed effortlessly. Industry experts have estimated that between 80%–90% of all e-commerce conducted on the internet is through adult sites.

Pornography in itself is debasing, but it is also a gross perversion of the truth because it focuses only on the physical act of sex and totally, utterly removes it from the covenant of marriage and the context of love. Added to which, pornography really is destructive and addictive. Why does pornography hold such fascination for people, men in particular? Partly, I believe, because it plays on mankind's naturally voyeuristic tendencies – a trait that is proven by the massive popularity of reality TV shows such as Big Brother, where we are invited to watch a group of people doing nothing for hours on end! And of course men tend to be visually stimulated more than women. But essentially, pornography is counterfeit intimacy. Every man and woman is looking for intimacy and will move in the direction that they believe will meet their needs. Pornography is a quick-fix, short cut to intimacy, but of course it is route that leads to a desperately poor caricature of the intimacy that God has prepared for us through the marriage covenant.

My advice to those who need to use email and internet on a daily basis, which is increasingly most of us, and who could be tempted to view adult sites, is to buy some effective filtering software that will block pornographic websites and ask a trusted friend or partner to enter the password on your behalf.

Base sexual talk

Keeping a purity to your language is so important to your purity as a whole. The things you say, especially if they are suggestive and full of innuendo can set an unhelpful train of thought in motion in someone else's mind. So much talk that is full of sexual innuendo takes place in the workplace that, as believers, we need to avoid participating in it and make a decision to be distinctively different.

Homosexual sin

The subject of homosexuality will be dealt with in a later chapter, but let me just note here that, if there is such a thing as heterosexual sin there must also be such a thing as homosexual sin. Unfortunately it has become so politically incorrect today to even mention that, but in a subsequent chapter we will look sympathetically at what God says about same sex relationships. I mention it here to keep the list complete.

What is the standard of God in all of this? Ephesians 5:3 says:

> *"But fornication and all uncleanness or covetousness, let it not even be named among you, as is fitting for saints."*

I really like the NIV version of the particular verse which says:

> *"But among you there must not even be a hint of sexual immorality, or of any kind of impurity, or of greed, because these are improper for God's holy people."*

Not even a hint of sexual immorality is God's standard. God doesn't want you to play so close to the edge that you are likely to fall over, even if you haven't fallen over yet. Why walk that close if you don't want to fall over? Walk somewhere that's safe instead.

How to Be Free from Sexual Sin

For the remainder of this chapter I want to give you six keys that will help you to break free from the bondage of sexual sin.

1. Make a decision

How do you get set free from sexual sin? First of all, as with any form of bondage, you need to *make a decision* that you want to be free. If you are in sexual bondage then you have to look honestly at what you have become and the damage that your sin is causing. How much of your life are you wasting by fighting sexual "fevers"? Do you long to be free from the sense of guilt and failure that your sexual sin produces in you?

The standard of God's Word, and what He wants for you, is for there to be "not even a hint" of sexual immorality in your life. So there is a decision to make and the stronger the decision you make, the easier it will be to get free. Instead of continually fighting off sinful sexual urges which sap your spiritual strength and divert you from your purpose, make a decision to be free and take the steps that follow.

2. Receive prayer and deliverance

Next you need to receive prayer and deliverance. I am not necessarily referring to deliverance from demonic forces, although demons often do attach themselves to habitual sexual sin and there can be a supernatural bondage there. But it is important that you receive prayer, and deliverance if necessary, and allow God to break the bondage in your life and bring healing and restoration to you.

3. Discipline yourself – learn new habits

Habits of the flesh need to be broken and the only way to do that is to discipline yourself to learn new habits. Especially for men, begin with "bouncing" your eyes away from any sexual image. It really can make a big difference. Normal God-given sexual desire *is manageable*, because we realise that there is a fire burning on the inside of every man! Whether he's a believer or an unbeliever, there is a fire there, we are no different! The thing to do is to keep the fire low. Don't deliberately pour fuel on the fire. If you walk into your office and you see a girl wearing a low-cut blouse, bounce your eyes immediately, because if you don't, you'll put fuel on your fire and by lunchtime you'll by totally distracted! However, you can control normal sexual desires that God has given you if you don't let them grow out of control. Don't make life tough for yourself. And ladies: watch your thought patterns. Bring then into line and don't let your emotions carry you away.

4. Engage in discipleship

Discipleship is a very important part in the process of getting free and staying free from sexual sin. Put another way, get yourself into mutually accountable relationships with other believers. Everyone needs others around them, regardless of their position or status, because no one is immune – that they can relate to honestly and pray with. Cell groups or prayer partners can be very beneficial in this regard because in them we can help each other, not as policemen but as fellow soldiers, to overcome our difficulties. If we are serious about the business of sexual purity then we also need to help one another.

5. Learn to walk in dignity

Sexual freedom is not about doing your own thing sexually – just whatever you feel like doing – it is about bringing your sexuality to order, to be harnessed for God's purposes. That is true sexual freedom, and when you walk in freedom it brings *dignity*. When your desires are under control, that makes a true man.

Being a man or woman of God is about taking the dignity that God bestows on His children and walking in that freedom. Learn to respect your dignity and that of others. Men, learn to respect women – respect them physically, emotionally and intellectually. Women, respect men – understand the differences, but don't exploit them.

6. Learn to walk in intimacy

Finally, learn to walk in intimacy. One of the biggest effects of sexual sin is that it robs us of dignity and intimacy. I've discovered in counselling men in particular who have sexual problems that every one of them speaks of a loss of intimacy. In other words, they have been seeking intimacy in the wrong way. Rather, focus on developing your intimacy with God so that when the time is right and it is time to "awaken love" (see Song of Solomon 2:7) you will be glad that you disciplined and prepared yourself to be a real blessing and a gift to your partner in marriage.

In the next chapter we will look at how to keep walking in sexual and emotional freedom.

CHAPTER SUMMARY

- God's gift of sex is part of His covenantal blessing to us and is designed to be use only within marriage. Any use of sex outside of those boundaries is a perversion of God's gift.
- The marriage covenant is unlike other human relationships in that the two people become ''one flesh'' or ''one person''. Sexual intimacy is the holy of holies of the expression of that companionship.
- Sex is a sacred act which is not to be taken outside the protection of the marriage relationship. Outside of its ''covering'' sex becomes a destructive force because it is a spiritual act as well as physical act and has spiritual consequences.
- Having understood God's framework we may define sexual sin as: any thought or act which is not directed in love to the fulfilment of your partner in marriage.
- There are four key areas we need to be aware of in order to exercise self-control over our sexuality and use it for God's glory: (1) love is the foundation and framework for sex; (2) guard your thought life and don't allow it to get out of control; (3) guard your emotions to protect yourself from vulnerability; (4) make sure your actions don't lead you into sexual sin.
- There are six steps to take to find freedom from sexual sin: (1) make a decision that you want to be free; (2) receive prayer and deliverance too if necessary; (3) discipline yourself to learn new habits; (4) engage in discipleship; (5) learn to walk in the dignity of God's freedom; (6) learn to walk in intimacy with God.

Walking in Sexual and Emotional Freedom

by Amanda Dye

What Is Sexual Freedom?

In looking at the topic of walking in sexual and emotional freedom it is appropriate to ask the question: "What is sexual freedom?" The world, of course, has a view on sexual freedom which is being free to do "what I want, when I want, without any interference from anyone else" – especially God. Because many view God as an authoritarian figure and a killjoy, they don't want to obey Him. But from a biblical point of view, we define sexual freedom as walking in obedience to God and being free from sexual sin.

In chapter 2 we read that God has high ideals for our sexuality. Because the Bible instructs us to do so, we have to, with God's help, attempt to walk and live out those ideals. We've also read that our sexuality is given to us by God so that we can bring emotional and sexual fulfilment to our partner in marriage. Your sexuality is not given for you alone; it is given so that you can bless and fulfil your partner. But this can seem to us as a narrow and extremely limited outlet for such a powerful drive as our sexuality, and it leaves many with questions.

For instance, what about the sexual and emotional needs of unmarried people? How do they handle their sexuality? We don't suddenly become sexual beings after we get married, as if we had no sexual thoughts, ideas or feelings before then and suddenly on our wedding night we discover we've got a sexual drive! It's not realistic to think that way. The Bible does caution us:

> *"Do not stir up nor awaken love*
> *Until it pleases."*
>
> (SONG OF SOLOMON 8:4)

However, our problem is trying to keep it asleep! How do you keep love asleep until it's appropriate to awaken it? If marriage is the only context for sexual fulfilment are we condemned to a life of sexual frustration before we get married? Stop and think about this for a moment. If you think along such lines, you are really saying, "My needs will not be met *until* I am married" or, "Marriage will bring me happiness and the complete fulfilment of all my needs."

Can that be true? No, of course it's not. These are clearly false expectations because marriage doesn't work like that and it was never God's intention for it to be that way. The purpose of marriage is not simply to meet one another's *every* need, and this is where many people have come unstuck. Many have entered into marriage with huge needs and have expected their partner to meet those needs. They have then been badly disappointed when they find that person cannot satisfy all their needs and desires. But the truth is, if you are not allowing God to meet your emotional needs, then your partner never will.

Wrong Expectations of Marriage

Rather than entering into marriage to have your needs met, you should enter marriage anticipating the joy of giving yourself to your partner to help to meet their needs and to be a gift and a blessing to them. Jesus said, it is more blessed to give than it is to receive. Many people are unhappy in their marriage because they have forgotten exactly that and are disappointed because they are not "getting out of it" what they expected.

People often get married because they are looking for security, significance and self-worth. Instead we should enter into marriage blessed and complete in Christ, ready to give of ourselves. Love is about giving and not getting. If you are reading this as a married person who feels that you are just not getting what you need from your marriage, begin to look at yourself and examine whether or not you have a love deficit in yourself. Look to see if you are *giving* to your partner as well as wanting to receive. Often when people address problems in their own life before God, they will see things improve dramatically in their marriage.

I don't believe that there is such a thing as an incompatible marriage. Once you are married you get on with it and it is compatible because as each partner walks with God, they get to know themselves and each other in Christ. In marriage you pledge to be the covenant partner of your husband or your wife. This means that you first find your fulfilment and your security in Christ and then you are free to love your husband/wife. If you're not whole in and of yourself, you cannot fully love. If you've got hurts, difficulties and experiences from your past that you have never given to Christ and received total healing from, then you are not free to love – those things will always surface and take up the space in your heart where love should be.

Each of us must learn to be complete in Christ. People who are in emotional or sexual bondage are not free to love as they should, because they are too focused on trying to get the other person to meet their needs. They become easily frustrated and annoyed when that doesn't happen and so they try harder to get what they're looking for. Finally, they can begin to look for it elsewhere and extra-marital relationships can be formed; they go looking for someone who will fill the love deficit in their hearts. This isn't the sort of love you need to heal a broken heart – that love only comes from God and He is able to heal those wounds.

So, it is very important to be complete as a single person, because if Jesus isn't enough for you when you're single, He certainly won't be enough for you when you're married. When you're married you've got another person to think about beside yourself. If Jesus hasn't met your needs as an individual, then you will find it all the more difficult when you are sharing your life with a partner who has his/her own needs. It's a recipe for disaster. You need to be whole in Christ before you give yourself to someone else.

Sexual Sin Can Be a Temptation for Married People as Well as Single People

Something that single Christians can find difficult to understand is that sexual sin is just as much a temptation for married people as it is for single people. Why is it today that so many marriages are failing? Why is the life-expectancy of many marriages so pessimistically short? It's because the temptation of sexual sin is no less potent for married couples than it is for single people. People who have not kept themselves pure before marriage generally have a tougher time remaining faithful to their marriage partner once they are married. That is why it is so important to deal with any sexual and emotional issues you may have before you get married. That way you will be able to build a stable and lasting marriage. Without that wholeness it will be a struggle.

Single people can put their sexual temptation down to the fact that they are not married and therefore cannot have sex. But sexual and emotional temptations are much deeper than that. The temptation to engage in sexual activity as a single Christian has a much deeper root than you might think. The sheer physical drive, the desires, the attractions, which we all have, and which are perfectly normal, are not what sexual temptation's all about.

Dealing with Sexual Temptation

Keeping our sex drive under control is not the major difficulty that each of us faces. It is our emotions that we struggle to deal with, rather than our hormones. It is damaged emotions and hurt that are the actual cause of people falling into sexual sin, as they go around looking for love and fulfilment in all the wrong places. The sexual drive in and of itself is a wholesome thing given to us by God, but only when your emotions are completely healed will you be able to view your sex drive from the right perspective.

We need therefore, with God's help, to learn how to deal with our emotional needs. The majority of sexual sin is a misguided pursuit of emotional fulfilment and satisfaction, and is not just about the thrill of orgasm. For men and women the issue is basically the same, although their emotional needs are different. Women are looking for romance, love, contentment and security; they want to find self-worth in a relationship. Men are looking for significance and self-value which they think they will gain through their conquest of a woman; sexual power is part of their desire to prove themselves as males.

Both men and women look for intimacy in different ways. They both commit the error of thinking that sex will provide them with it. But sex on its own as a physical act will never provide anyone with the satisfaction that he/she desires. It may be pleasant for a time, but it won't bring fulfilment. Sex is designed as a way of *expressing intimacy*, not a way of getting it. Sex without real, relational intimacy is merely a physical and biological act.

Sex is an act that can produce intense, physical sensations, but these do not produce lasting emotional fulfilment and satisfaction – it's a short-lived thrill. Having sex outside of marriage has worse effects for believers than it does for non-believers, in the sense that it brings guilt into the equation. If you are following God and trying to obey His commands and you succumb to sexual temptation and fall, then the guilt and shame of having done that will only add to the dissatisfaction you feel – that it was short-lived and didn't fulfil you emotionally as you expected.

The author and Christian psychologist, Dr John White, writes:

> "Sex [within marriage] was intended to end aloneness. The communication, the closeness, the intimacy, the knowing and being known, the loving and being loved, is a complex living structure that takes years to grow. It began as a delicate and beautiful plant, vibrant with life. It grows into a sturdy tree with deep roots to sustain it through the drought and the storm."

That's what sex inside marriage is: two whole people in relationship with one another where the sexual intimacy of that relationship helps it to continue to grow and develop. That is why it is so important to resist the urges of sexual temptation and preserve ourselves for the precious, intimate relationship that lies ahead.

Finding Emotional Fulfilment and Freedom in Christ

Your emotions point to inner needs that are either being met or not being met. We all have emotional needs and we look to have them met in many different ways. A variety of factors will dictate how you in particular go about seeking to have your emotional needs met, depending on factors such as your life experiences, where you come from, what your parents were like, what your childhood was like etc. All the experiences of your life will combine to make you look for a particular kind of emotional fulfilment. For instance, if you came from a very unstable home, looking for security and stability will be high on your emotional agenda. If you have experienced a number of loveless relationships, then you will be looking for love and affirmation as a priority.

The most important thing for us to learn is, there is only one way to have all our emotional needs met: to come to Jesus, to receive healing, and to truly know who we are in Him. There is no other way. You can travel the world seeking fulfilment, seeking relationships, pursuing different careers, seeking many things, but you will never find fulfilment until you discover who you are in Christ.

Positive and negative emotions

All of us have both positive and negative emotions. Experiencing positive emotions points to the fact that our needs are being met. When our needs are fulfilled we will experience:

- Joy
- Peace

- Fulfilment
- Contentment

If you experience these emotions then it means you are a healthy believer and you know who you are in Christ. Negative emotions however, reveal that we have needs that are not being met and we are unsure of our true identity in Christ. Such negative emotions include:

- Fear
- Anger
- Frustration
- Depression
- Emptiness
- Sadness

Many people in their desperation for emotional fulfilment have rushed into relationships or into marriage, believing that their partner will meet all their needs. They have not stopped to consider whether this person is actually the life-partner that God intended for them. But once in the relationship, or worse still the marriage, what do they find? They find that their emotional needs are just as great as ever and they now have the added problem of worrying about the future stability of their relationship.

The good news . . .

The good news is that God can meet all your needs. Your deep basic needs for security, significance and self-worth, are all met in Jesus, and He alone can accomplish that.

At this point you may be thinking, "Well actually, I am

not a particularly needy person. I come from very good family, I had lots of love, affirmation and security." Well, praise God for that. Even so, you as an individual still need to know your place and your position in Jesus Christ. Before you enter into marriage you still need to know who you are in Christ and be fully secure in that identity.

Until you know what it is to have your needs met in Christ at a deep and not a superficial level, you will never be satisfied and fulfilled as a person. You will always be looking over the garden fence thinking, "The grass is greener on that side of the fence. Their lawn looks greener than mine!" You will always be dissatisfied as long as you feel that someone else has something that you don't have.

But in John 10:10 Jesus makes this amazing promise to us:

> *"The thief does not come except to steal, and to kill, and to destroy. I have come that they may have life, and that they may have it more abundantly."*
>
> (John 10:10)

Jesus came to give us *complete life*. He didn't just come to give us spiritual life (although that is of critical importance), He came to make us whole people – body, soul and spirit. God desires each of us to be made completely whole in Him. The difficulty is that many people are happy for Jesus to be their Saviour, but they are less willing for Him to be Lord of every part of their lives. Unless He is Lord of every area of your life however, He cannot heal your emotions and make you a whole person. You have to allow Him to be not just your Saviour, but your Healer and Deliverer too.

The thief has indeed stolen and destroyed much of our peace, joy and fulfilment by enticing us to seek it in the wrong places, for the wrong reasons, and with the wrong people. That is Satan's ploy. He hates healthy, wholesome, Christian families. If you are active for God in ministry then you are a threat to him and he doesn't like it. He will use any deception he can to target you and bring disunity into your life to take away your joy and fulfilment.

A fulfilled person is not just a happy person; he or she is a very attractive person. They stand out from the crowd because they are attractive on the inside. It's not just how they look externally – an emotionally whole person is attractive on every level. If you are fulfilled in Christ and at peace with yourself, you will attract your partner-to-be like a bee to honey. When you are a beautiful, whole person, people will be knocking on your door, wanting to know more about you because you'll be so attractive! Ladies, you won't have to go out looking for the men, they will be on your doorstep saying, "Please, can I take you out to dinner ... please, please!" It's possible when you allow Jesus to have total control and fulfil you emotionally.

The Trap of Counterfeit Love

A consistent ploy of the enemy is to look for areas of vulnerability in our lives and deliberately target them. He looks to see where we have emotional deficits and then subtly "suggests" ways in which we could meet those needs. Needless to say these are wrong ways that won't ultimately result in our fulfilment, but further bondage.

This is how it happens, and I base this story on the typical case of a teenage girl:

A girl grows up never really feeling that her father affirms her. Her home is fine, but her self-worth is really lacking. Surprisingly, this girl is a Christian and comes from a strong Christian family. As she enters adulthood, she never feels satisfied with herself or her life, and so she begins to search elsewhere for the approval she has always craved from her father. Her problem is simply that she has a father-love deficit. She has been wounded by her Dad's seeming lack of approval of her as a person and she has never sought healing in this area.

When someone has this kind of vulnerability, especially a believer, then the devil is on their doorstep in no time to tell them that it is possible to have male-approval – for a price. Satan loves this kind of situation because it is an opportunity for him to spread his deception. He says, "Of course you can have male approval, provided you do it my way." His aim of course is to entice people into sexual sin.

The pain in this girl's heart is so intense that she gives in, first to one sexual experience with a man, and then another, and another. She drifts from one loveless physical relationship to another in the hope of finding the affirmation she so badly needs, but she never finds it.

That is bad enough, but for many young girls, it often doesn't end there. Many have ended up in prostitution because of the wounds of a father-love deficit in their life. Satan wants to rob every person of the joy and fulfilment that can be theirs in Christ, and so he tries hard to ensnare us in bondage through sexual sin.

What this girl really needed was paternal love, not sex (which she was deceived into thinking would bring her love and affirmation), but Satan tricked her into believing that all male love is the same and can be bought. That is a common lie of the enemy. This young girl desperately wanted to obey God, but her emotional pain overwhelmed her. Satan managed to trigger the volcano that was just waiting to erupt and she jumped at the chance for love, even if it was counterfeit love.

How to Keep Pure

With all the emotional ups and downs of life and the pressure we face in modern society, how then does one keep pure and walk in emotional and sexual freedom? There are a number of common sense things you can do that will help.

First, you can help yourself by not reading many of today's popular magazines that are a flimsy excuse for pornography. The current trend for mass market "lifestyle" magazines is to have articles on sex from beginning to end – the "top ten tips for a better sex life" etc. Such features are an excuse to display many explicit pictures, along with no-holds barred write-ups that go into great detail.

Secondly, you can help yourself by not watching movies that also are nothing more than glorified pornography and which underwrite and "approve" of casual sexual relationships. If you do watch such movies or TV programmes then all that will happen is your sex drive will be stimulated and you will begin to focus more on more about how you might go about satisfying those urges.

Thirdly, in Ephesians 4:22–23 Paul tells us that when we become new creatures in Christ we must "put off" our old life and the lifestyle that accompanied it and follow Christ completely. Of course that means receiving wholeness and healing in Christ, but it also means we must be vigilant about our lifestyle to ensure that we don't slip into bad habits which are alien to our new life in Christ.

Fourthly, don't try to fill emotional voids in your life with anything other than God. The topic of this book is sexuality, so I have focused on that area, but there are many other things that people use to try to "heal" themselves emotionally, instead of allowing Jesus to do it. It could be money, power, success, ambition. Whatever we focus on, other than God, to bring fulfilment pushes God into second place. The thing that is driving us, whatever it may be, becomes an idol in our life and eventually will take us over completely. Jesus must be at the centre of your life as Lord and Saviour. If He's not, then you are living in disobedience to God. Partial obedience is no obedience at all.

Many have made their relationship with another person their idol. It has become of paramount importance in their life, rather than God. As soon as we find someone who eases our loneliness and emptiness, we become addicted to it. Suddenly we "can't live without them" and we talk about them all day long. Yes, it can be a beautiful, pure, love relationship as God intended – but very often it isn't. It's trying to have your needs met in the wrong way. If the relationship doesn't work out, then you will end up being wounded.

If you are a person who is living with guilt from the past, maybe because you've had a string of relationships, or have been trapped in some kind of sexual sin, I want to tell you that you don't have to continue carrying that guilt. Jesus loves you, He died for you, and He has forgiveness for you if you will just come to Him and release the burden into His hands.

If, after praying, you still feel the pain and are troubled, then you may need to seek some assistance through counselling, but God will make you whole if you desire it. God will heal every wound if you let Him touch every area of your life.

We carry around a lot of baggage with us because we are often not prepared to trust God with every part of our lives. If we don't trust Him totally, then we will be inclined to snatch certain areas of our life back from Him – just in case we don't like how He handles them. Jesus wants to heal you, but you have to give Him permission to do so. The blood of Jesus can cleanse you from any area of impurity, and set you free from any area you are struggling with. Find a quiet place today, and release to Him all those hurts of the past and the things you have done that you are ashamed of, and His mercy and grace will touch your life and bring healing.

Chapter Summary

- True sexual freedom is defined as walking in obedience to God and being free from sexual sin.
- God has high ideals for our sexuality and with His help we can live out those ideals – to preserve our sexuality exclusively for blessing our marriage partner.
- Many enter marriage with wrong expectations of what it will do for them. They look for it to give them security, significance and self-worth, but only Christ can fulfil those needs perfectly.
- Rather we should enter marriage emotionally whole, ready to give of ourselves to our partner. If Jesus isn't enough for you when you are single, then He won't be enough for you when you are married.
- Sexual sin is just as much a temptation for married people as it is for single people. But keeping our sex drive under control is not the greatest challenge we face. We must look to the root causes of sexual sin – damaged emotions.
- Emotions point to inner needs that are not being met. We need to learn to come to Jesus to receive healing and to know who we are in Him. The good news is, Jesus can meet all of your needs and give you a "complete" life.
- Be aware of the devil's trap of counterfeit love and avoid falling for it. Don't make idols of your relationships, but focus on God.

WHAT GOD SAYS ABOUT SAME SEX RELATIONSHIPS – PART ONE

The debate about same sex relationships is one that has been the source of much controversy in recent times, and continues to stir heated emotions on both sides of the divide. Recently in the United States homosexual marriages have been made legal and there are moves in the United Kingdom to pass similar legislation in the form of same sex union contracts. The question is, what does God have to say about all of this?

At either end of the spectrum of opinion, most people's minds are already made up. They either take a liberal or a legalistic view of events. The liberals are bound to say that anything goes and God loves us all anyway, so it doesn't really matter. The legalists will insist that God is about to zap all homosexuals and lesbians at any moment and burn them off the face of the planet. I just wonder really if God is not a little embarrassed by both these views?

Rather than get involved with the fringe issues of the debate, we ought to examine what the Word of God has to say, for that is the compass for all believers to be guided by. Rather than being silent on the issue, as so many claim, the Bible actually gives us many examples of same sex relationships; they are positive portrayals of how same sex relationships were designed by God to function.

Naomi and Ruth

The whole story of the book of Ruth is centred around a friendship between Naomi and Ruth. Ruth was Naomi's daughter-in-law; Naomi's son, Ruth's husband, was dead. Because her son was no longer alive, Naomi wanted to release Ruth to go and find a new life, so she said to her, "I'm going back to Bethlehem. There's nothing there for you, so you had better go back to your family. Go back to your home." But, in words which are some of the most beautiful in the Bible, Ruth replies:

"Entreat me not to leave you,
Or to turn back from following after you;
For wherever you go, I will go;
And wherever you lodge, I will lodge;
Your people shall be my people,
And your God, my God."

(Ruth 1:16)

What a wonderful pledge Ruth made to Naomi! It was a statement of relationship and of covenant. Ruth did indeed follow Naomi and the whole story reveals a number of insights into how same sex relationships are really meant to function. A godly same sex relationship, such as this, will result in a number of things:

Close friends

First of all we see that God blesses close relationships between members of the same sex and they can result in close friendships. Although there was an age difference between the two women, they became good friends and they were a blessing to one another.

Cross-generational mentoring

The women's relationship also had an aspect of mentoring to it. Although Naomi was Ruth's mother-in-law, their relationship became much more like that of mother and daughter. Naomi could offer Ruth guidance, nurture and mentoring that would help her to mature as a woman. It would be wonderful if every woman in the Church of Jesus Christ had a similar spiritual mother figure to draw from, in the same way that many guys have spiritual father figures.

Covenantal

Surprisingly perhaps, the Bible does not say that the marriage covenant is the only covenant there is. People of the same sex can have a covenantal relationship too that works towards the purposes of God for each person's life. Naomi and Ruth's relationship was covenantal in nature. It was more than being "friends", Ruth had made a promise to Naomi – a promise of faithfulness that she would never abandon her, come what may. Naomi and Ruth did not have just a "selfish" friendship whereby they simply enjoyed each other's company – it was more than that – it was godly; their relationship was good and it looked towards the purposes of God – it wasn't inward looking and self-seeking as so many modern relationships are.

There are two further things that stand out about Naomi and Ruth's relationship:

1. It was not a denial of marriage

This relationship was neither a denial of marriage, nor a substitute for it. It certainly wasn't a modification of God's covenant of marriage either. In fact, it ultimately led to a marriage as Boaz came on the scene and a wonderful love story began to develop which eventually brought Boaz and Ruth together.

2. It was part of God's plan to bring Christ into the world

Throughout this story God is working out His purposes through the lives of these characters, because all these events were an important part of God's overall plan to reveal Christ to the world. What a great objective to have for your friendship!

Look at this amazing sequence of events: Ruth met Boaz, they got married, and they had a baby whose name was Obed. Obed was the father of Jesse, who was the father of David, and David was the royal dynasty out of which came Jesus the Christ. Naomi and Ruth's relationship was so yielded to God that it became part of the plan and purpose of God to reveal Christ to the world!

David and Jonathan

Another amazing example of a same sex relationship, this time between two men, is found in the biblical account of David and Jonathan. Looking at their relationship it is immediately evident that it was completely in line with God's messianic purposes and the establishment of the Davidic dynasty. It paints a very positive picture of a same sex relationship – all the more so because this relationship was theologically significant. Again, it was about much more than two people being friends, sharing together and enjoying one another's company – as great as that is. God blessed their friendship and out of that covenant He revealed His kingdom to the world.

Just like Naomi and Ruth, the relationship between David and Jonathan was not a substitute for marriage. Marriage is God's chief covenant of companionship, designed to be fruitful and produce multiplication, but it does not preclude the possibility of same sex friendships which can be so precious and important. It is really important that we all have close relationships with people of the same gender, where we can enjoy great fellowship before the Lord. Everyone should have that blessing.

When you examine the relationship that David and Jonathan had, a number of key passages stand out. The first is found in 1 Samuel chapter 18:

> *"Now when he had finished speaking to Saul, the soul of Jonathan was knit to the soul of David, and Jonathan loved him as his own soul. Saul took him that day, and would not let him go home to his father's house anymore. Then Jonathan and David made a covenant, because he loved him as his own soul. And Jonathan took off the robe that was on him and gave it to David, with his armour, even to his sword and his bow and his belt."*
>
> (1 SAMUEL 18:1–4)

You will not find a more touching, more affirming, or a more blessed picture of a same sex relationship anywhere. I don't think God could speak any louder or more clearly than this: He is saying that He honours and blesses committed same sex relationships which are submitted to His purpose and His will.

The language of Scripture is very strong and intense. Jonathan's soul was *"knit to the soul of David and Jonathan loved him as his own soul."* Because of the incredibly strong bond that was established between them, they made a covenant and later on that covenant was extended, as we shall see.

As the story progresses we see that King Saul, Jonathan's father, becomes progressively jealous of David. David is rapidly becoming more popular than the king himself and the people are recognising, perhaps even exaggerating, his exploits in battle:

"So the women sang as they danced, and said:

'Saul has slain his thousands,
and David his ten thousands.' "

(1 SAMUEL 18:7)

This incenses Saul who angrily responds:

"They have ascribed to David ten thousands, and to me they have ascribed only thousands. Now what more can he have but the kingdom?"

(1 SAMUEL 18:8)

We read that, from that moment on, Saul kept an eye on David and even looked for opportunities to kill him. He may well have succeeded if it were not for the intervention of Jonathan. Jonathan decided that he would warn David of any impending danger, so that he would be prepared for it, and could escape unharmed. At the beginning of 1 Samuel chapter 19 we read:

"Now Saul spoke to Jonathan his son and to all his servants, that they should kill David; but Jonathan, Saul's son, delighted greatly in David. So Jonathan told David, saying, 'My father Saul seeks to kill you. Therefore please be on your guard until morning, and stay in a secret place and hide.' "

(1 SAMUEL 19:1–2)

This is incredible, given that Jonathan is Saul's son! With hindsight we now know that what Jonathan was doing was helping to preserve the one who was anointed to be king.

Naturally speaking, Jonathan should have been the one who inherited and led this great dynasty. He could have become king, and yet he was not concerned about his own position and status. Rather his concern was for his friend, whom he loved, and whom he recognised had God's hand upon his life.

So Jonathan intervened and warned David that his life was in danger. The situation became so severe that David was forced to flee for his life and go into exile. At this point the friends were forced to part and they swore an oath to their friendship and commitment to one another:

> "*. . . David arose from a place toward the south, fell on his face to the ground, and bowed down three times. And they kissed one another; and they wept together, but David more so. Then Jonathan said to David, 'Go in peace, since we have both sworn in the name of the* Lord, *saying, "May the* Lord *be between you and me, and between your descendants and my descendants, forever."' So he arose and departed, and Jonathan went into the city.*"
>
> (1 Samuel 20:41–42)

David and Jonathan obviously had a deep relationship. There are several aspects about their relationship which are similar to the relationship between Naomi and Ruth, which we ought to note:

First of all, they were *close friends* and they had a love for one another that resulted in a *covenant.* Their love covenant caused each to put the other person first. As far as we can tell from Scripture, the two men were of a *similar age* (unlike Naomi and Ruth) and so effectively were like brothers. Their relationship was very *intense*, and it was *multi-generational.* David and Jonathan's relationship survived into future generations. After Jonathan was tragically killed in battle, and David was established as king in the place of Saul, David called for any relatives of the house of Jonathan to come forth so that he could honour his pledge to bless Jonathan's descendants. One son of Jonathan, a man called Mephiboshesh who was lame, was discovered, and David sought him out and showed love to him for the sake of Jonathan. Finally, David and Jonathan's relationship *served the purposes of God.* It wasn't selfish. Jonathan saved David's life even though he knew it would prevent him from becoming king.

I wish in our modern culture we understood friendship, loyalty and love like that. We'd be much healthier as human beings, and much more of a witness for Jesus Christ if we had more David-Jonathan, Naomi-Ruth type relationships.

The Uniqueness of Marriage

The covenant of marriage is first mentioned in Genesis 2:24:

> *"Therefore a man shall leave his father and mother and be joined to his wife, and they shall become one flesh."*

This original covenant of companionship was given by God in the context of the great creation mandate to fill the earth and to subdue it; to multiply and have dominion. It was a covenant of complete companionship at every level, including the physical, sexual level. But it cannot be compared with the covenant of companionship that one can enjoy with a person of the same sex – that companionship operates on an entirely different level.

The marriage covenant necessarily entails two people of the opposite sex being "joined together" and becoming "one flesh" in the context of sexual intimacy – which God has only ever sanctioned and blessed within the confines of marriage. No other relationship can be a substitute for that. The blessing of sexually intimate union is not given to:

- mother/daughter relationships
- father/son relationships
- mother/son relationships
- daughter/father relationships
- brother/sister relationships
- relationships between special friends of the same sex
- relationships between special friends of the opposite sex

The Boundaries of Same Sex Relationships

The Bible is very clear about this. Sexual intimacy is solely for a husband and wife within the bounds of marriage. What this clearly tells us is that there are boundaries in same sex relationships that must not be crossed. To some readers this may seem obvious, but to many this very fact is a stumbling block, since society has so strongly promoted the view that freedom only comes through the *removal* of boundaries.

For many, the way to have fun is to do whatever you want with whoever you want, without any boundaries. But the truth is, in our relationships with God and each other, the real blessing is released when we operate within God-given boundaries.

The boundaries of same sex relationships are this: no matter how deep or intense or loving the relationship is (and we have seen that such relationships can be so powerful as to extend beyond the grave and span generations to come), there is no evidence in Scripture – taking even the most sympathetic view – that any form of sexual expression can be sanctioned between people of the same sex.

There are many examples of love and closeness between members of the same sex in the Bible, but not one of them has any sexual connotations.

John the beloved disciple rested on the breast of Jesus at the Last Supper. Such a physical expression of love reveals a deep friendship, even a level of intimacy that some friends would not be comfortable with. But it would be wrong to move from such signs of affection (the Greek *philos* love) to homoerotic acts (the Greek *eros* love).[1] For people who see that in the relationship between Jesus and John, it tells us more about them than it does about Jesus and John. We must be careful not to read into the Bible what isn't there, or what we would like to be there.

I remember one young man that I taught and trained in Bible college many years ago. He turned away from the Lord and left Bible college in order to express himself in a homosexual relationship. I've kept in touch with him down through the years and spoken to him frequently. Never once have I condemned him; never once have I made him feel bad as if I would in some way judge his life. I continue to offer the love and friendship that I would offer anybody because

God has called us not to condemn, but to love people; to understand what their issues are. But in a moment of truth I asked him, "Have you changed your understanding of life to meet your need to express this lifestyle?" And he said, "Honestly, yes. That's what I have done."

Another example of "closeness" that is sometimes misinterpreted is the story of the centurion who had a sick servant in Luke chapter 7, which portrays a different kind of closeness. The Bible says that the centurion had a servant "whom he loved". The word "love" is used, but there is no evidence whatsoever that the centurion had a sexual relationship with his slave. Some liberal theologians who would like to push a gay agenda have tried to argue that historically, that would have been a normal thing to have happened, but no matter how clever a historian you are, you have to import something into that text in order to imply there was a sexual relationship between the two.

So, the Bible includes many strong expressions of love, even of physical contact, but they always stop short of erotic intimacy. It is physical closeness, but *never* sexual. What a pity that physical closeness between people of the same sex has been so "sexualised" in modern society. The modern world cannot comprehend a level of physical closeness without an underlying sexual agenda. That's a tragedy. Today, for example, adults who have a pure and genuine fondness for children are afraid to express their care for fear of being branded paedophiles. It seems that the enemy has managed to spoil even the most innocent of relationships by pointing the finger and trying to raise the issue of sex.

So the Bible is clear about the fact that same sex relationships are intended for friendship, companionship, mutual encouragement, and to fulfil the purposes of God. In the next chapter we will examine more closely why the Bible insists that same sex relationships that go beyond the boundaries of Naomi-Ruth or David-Jonathan type relationships are outside of God's plan for humanity.

Chapter Summary

- People have tended to hold extreme views on same sex relationships: liberal or legalistic. But the Bible provides many positive examples of how God made same sex relationships to function.
- A godly same sex relationship (as demonstrated in the relationship between Ruth and Naomi) will have the following elements: (1) close friendship; (2) a mentoring aspect; (3) a covenant of companionship.
- Biblical same sex relationships are not a denial of marriage, nor a substitute for it. Many same sex relationships in the Bible were key to establishing God's plans and purposes in the world.
- The covenant of marriage is unique and cannot be compared with the covenant of companionship that members of the same sex can enjoy.
- The Bible is clear that sexual intimacy is for marriage only and has no place within same sex relationships.

CHAPTER 6

WHAT GOD SAYS ABOUT SAME SEX RELATIONSHIPS – PART TWO

OUTSIDE OF GOD'S PLAN

Scripture teaches that sex outside of the marriage covenant is outside the plan of God. That includes sexual acts between members of the same sex, as well as sexual acts between members of different sexes. There are a number of biblical passages that explicitly forbid sex between members of the same sex. The first, in Leviticus chapter 20, could not be clearer:

> *"If a man lies with a male as he lies with a woman, both of them have committed an abomination. They shall surely be put to death. Their blood shall be upon them."*
>
> (Leviticus 20:13)

At the time when this command was given by God, Levitical law was the law of the land. The people were living in an era where religion and the state were the same thing; religious laws were state laws and vice versa. When Jesus came He changed all of that. Jesus said (in relation to taxation), *"Render therefore to Caesar the things that are Caesar's, and to God the things that are God's"* (Matthew 22:21). What He did was to separate Church and state.

Some people say, therefore, that Levitical law is completely irrelevant to the homosexual debate because it governed arcane ceremonies and legal issues that related to *state law* and not *moral law*. Such verses as Leviticus 20:13 are seen as irrelevant because they are to do with "religious" and not "moral" issues. Despite such views however, we notice that three verses earlier the law forbids adultery, which is clearly a moral issue. It says:

> *"The man who commits adultery with another man's wife, he who commits adultery with his neighbour's wife, the adulterer and the adulteress, shall surely be put to death."*
>
> (Leviticus 20:10)

What this tells us is that both homosexual sin and heterosexual sin are *sin* in God's eyes – there is no difference. The Bible condemns heterosexual sin and homosexual sin evenly and equally. God's ideal for sexuality is the fulfilment of a husband/wife in marriage only. Anything outside of that is unacceptable.

Of course, these texts are not to be used as rods upon people's backs to beat them down, and especially not for heterosexual "sinners" to condemn homosexual "sinners" with a self-righteous attitude. That is a hypocrisy in the Church that I want to expose! I do so out of gentleness because I want to foster an attitude in which believers welcome everyone to come and find Christ, because all have sinned and fall short of the glory of God.

However, both these Leviticus verses do deal with moral issues. Some have tried to get around the issue by claiming that the homosexual practices condemned in Scripture relate to ancient pagan practices of idolatrous worship and ritualistic prostitution involving "religious" acts of immorality such as fertility rites and so on. Indeed there was a pagan religion that existed throughout the Bible, which was opposed by the prophets, in which people engaged in sexual acts as a form of ritual worship in honour of pagan gods – and homosexuality was part of that, I agree. But we have to examine the whole of Scripture to see its teaching in balance, and Paul's teaching in Romans chapter 1 clearly shows that such deviations from God's standards are "unnatural" and sinful. Paul doesn't just condemn homosexual and lesbian acts out of hand though, he goes further by talking about the downward spiral that the people who commit such acts will suffer, unless they experience God's mercy and grace through Jesus Christ. This applies to all sin of course and not just homosexual sin. The list of sins Paul is speaking about in Romans 1 shows that homosexual sin is not set apart as some particularly gross sin in God's sight. God hates all sin.

Later in 1 Corinthians 6:9–11 Paul writes:

> *"Do you not know that the unrighteous will not inherit the kingdom of God? Do not be deceived. Neither fornicators, nor idolaters, nor adulterers, nor homosexuals, nor sodomites, nor thieves, nor covetous, nor drunkards, nor revilers, nor extortioners will inherit the kingdom of God."*

Here he is speaking about some general descriptions of the works of the flesh and he includes amongst them both the *active* and *passive* actions of male homosexuality. The Greek word for homosexual in this passage is *malkos* which is translated as "soft to the touch" – metaphorically speaking "effeminate" – and refers to the passive partner in a homosexual relationship or "catomite". A catomite is the opposite of a sodomite, in other words the one who receives the penis in his anus. Later in the same verse Paul highlights the "active" party in a homosexual relationship, the sodomite (Greek: *arsenokoites*). Some may be shocked by the degree of explicit detail found in this verse. But God is explicit concerning the things He will not tolerate.

So, although we may find it shocking, God is not shocked by what people do. God can accurately and lovingly describe the wrong way and the right way to use our bodies. The good news is that through Christ we can be transformed and set free. As Paul points out:

> *"Such were some of you. But you were washed, but you were sanctified, but you were justified in the name of the Lord Jesus and by the Spirit of our God."*
>
> (1 CORINTHIANS 6:11)

Let no one tell you otherwise! God has the power to wash, cleanse and remove every contamination from this sin and every other sin, because the blood of Jesus Christ is all-powerful. That's good news for all of us, because we all need to be washed in the blood of Jesus and have our sins removed.

ARE PEOPLE "BORN" GAY, OR DO THEY "CHOOSE" TO BE GAY?

Perhaps the hottest issue currently under debate is that of gender orientation. Many people today hold the view that homosexuality, for instance, is "natural" for some people and that means we have no right to judge them. Well, we have no right to judge them anyway! Our job as believers is to love and accept people, but that doesn't mean to say that we must approve of their lifestyles. Love and approval are not exactly the same thing.

The real question that people are asking is, "Are people born gay or do they choose to become gay?" It is the "nature versus nurture" argument. People will argue that it is impossible for a person to change their basic sexual orientation and that we have no right to expect them to do so. One book that examines this subject very deeply and studies the medical, scientific facts – not trying to make a case, but simply presenting the results of the studies that have been done – says this:

> "It is clear that although individuals differ in the strength of their impulses because of many variables – some genetic, most not – do not fully account for activity, homosexual activity included."[1]

In other words, science tells us that whilst there may be some forms of genetic bias, genetic tendency or predisposition (there *may be* – it's not proven), there is absolutely no proof whatsoever that a person is *born* gay. That kind of evidence is utterly and completely missing. Yet I could take you to the popular bookshelves of our stores and show you books that categorically say the opposite. One book makes the statement, "People are born gay in the same way that some people are born with blue eyes and others with brown eyes." Quite simply, they are lying. Being "born gay" is not established as a fact and this is something that the aggressive homosexual lobby is determined to keep from the public through so-called political correctness. This kind of popular opinion is fuelled by the media who have reported on dubious studies that claim to find homosexuality to be genetic, or as *Time* magazine once put it, "Born gay". But there's no such thing as the "gay gene".

The motivation behind identifying "gayness" as genetic is simple: if it is genetic then it can no longer be determined to be a moral issue. After all, if it's in your genes then you can't help it, right? But, as another writer put it, "We should see the fallacy in the claim that homosexuality is not immoral because it is (supposedly) genetic . . . [it] is certainly false as a scientific statement . . . " And it is also a false conclusion to say, "Science has proved homosexuality is right" because science has nothing to say about morality. You cannot prove by scientific means whether something is morally "right" or "wrong".

Homosexuality is a complex human experience and none of it fits into a predetermined pattern. One thing that I find ridiculous is when Christians treat people who are struggling with issues of homosexuality as those who've simply decided to be gay – as if one day they got out of bed in the morning and said, "I'm going to be gay." It doesn't happen that way. There is always a complex set of circumstances that brings a person to that point. It does involve personal choice as well, of course, don't mistake that; but apart from cases of rape or sexual abuse, homosexual acts are chosen, not forced upon others. And even in the cases where a person has been violated against their will that does not automatically mean the abused person becomes a homosexual. Homosexuality is far more complicated than that.

Many people speak of their homosexuality as always having been with them; they have been aware of an attraction to people of the same sex as long as they can remember. What factors might be contributing to this perception that people have? There are at least four:

1. Whilst science does not prove that people are born gay, there may be a predisposition towards gayness, in the same way that people who are very tall and athletic would be predisposed to becoming good basketball

players. Whether they become what they are predisposed to however, depends on a whole range of other factors, it's not simply due to their disposition; they need a motive and an opportunity to choose to go down that road.

2. There may be a biological component in the mix of factors leading a person to have a homosexual inclination and hence, a homosexual lifestyle. One theory states that hormonal influences in the womb account for some "feminine" characteristics in men and some "masculine" characteristics in women. Some offer this as an explanation for homosexuality.
3. Others speak of psychological factors, either in infancy (such as in the theories of Freud) or in a person's upbringing. One theory addresses the issue of a person's psychosexual development. It states that the parent of the opposite sex to the person is particularly important in the early years of a child's development, helping the child to gain a healthy view of the opposite sex for later in life. In adolescence however, it is said that the same sex parent is important for the discovery of your own sexual identity as a male or a female. If these relationships are not present or are dysfunctional during these critical years of development, then homosexuality can be the result. But nothing in these theories have ever proven that people are "made" gay by their psychological or environmental history, although these may be strong influences.
4. There can be a misunderstanding about the basis of our free will. We should understand that God has given us the dignity of freewill and that we are *morally responsible* human

> beings. This means that no matter what influences are upon us – whether cultural, environmental, or biological – they do not remove our right to choose our lifestyle or the freedom to live it out.

People who have homosexual tendencies are still people with the power of choice – to live in one way or another. No one is forced to live in a certain way, but chooses to do so. No one has the right to judge another because of their sexual orientation or to take the view that they are better or worse than the next person. What is needed among believers today is love, humility and compassion to reach out to those who are struggling and offer help. Jesus can and will save all those who trust in Him, and He can also deliver us from the hold that sin has on our lives. This doesn't mean that every sinful desire is removed, but the power of that sin is broken and can no longer have a hold over us.

The Shape of Holiness

Let's now move on and ask the question, "What does holiness mean in all of this?" There are people out there who say they have been "shaped" by various factors which have led to their particular sexual orientation, and they are looking for answers. They have a belief in and a love for God and a desire to live as a Christian, but they struggle with their sexuality and particularly their attraction to members of the same sex. What does holiness mean to them? I believe there are three important issues that need to be understood:

1. You are not defined by your sexual orientation

The term "homosexual" wasn't even coined or used more than a hundred and fifty years ago. You need not be defined by such a "label". Many people speak of their basic sexual orientation being completely unaltered even after many years of study, prayer, fasting, counselling and deliverance. You name it, they've had it – but they still have that *tendency* in their life. But, I want to tell you, if that is you today, you don't have to define yourself by your tendencies. What kind of mad world does that? We are beings made in the image of God and we are fully human in every part of our lives – the sexual side being just one part. We have certain "tendencies" in many aspects of life, but when your life is yielded to the Holy Spirit it is possible to have control over them.

2. You do have to resist temptation and not give in to it

Every Christian is faced with this situation, regardless of what the sin is. We all have temptations, we all have desires that God doesn't approve of, and we've got to say no to them. If somebody is struggling with homosexual desires, they're probably sitting next to somebody else who's struggling with heterosexual desires. If you walk through any London Tube station you will see posters displaying the semi-naked bodies of men and women. Which of those images attracts you is the nature of your battle. In the final analysis, both people are struggling with images of naked people! So, let's not put people into special categories. At the end of the day we are all fighting the same battle – the battle against the flesh. All of us can be victorious over the sin in our lives.

3. You need to deal with the issue at root level

Any issue relating to sin needs to be dealt with at root level, not just at the behavioural level. I believe the Church of Jesus Christ doesn't understand this fully enough. We should know, because Jeremiah prophesied and said, *"The heart is deceitful above all things, and desperately wicked"* (Jeremiah 17:9), that people can change their outward behaviour and yet their heart remains the same. Unless your heart is changed, the change in your behaviour doesn't cut any ice with God. We therefore need to look deeper than just the external habits and practices associated with different forms of sinning for the answers we seek. Many approaches to holiness are superficial, because sin is seen only as "wrong acts" that the individual has deliberately chosen to commit. But sin is much deeper than simply "bad behaviour", it is a state of the heart that must be dealt with.

In life, we are all looking for basically the same things: security, significance, self-worth, friendship, love, affirmation, acceptance. Those are the common needs of every human being. How we search for the answers to those needs varies with almost every individual. The story of how you, before you came to Christ, sought to meet your needs, and my story, will be very different – but in a greater sense they are the same story. People who struggle today with certain behaviour patterns can trace back to root level the deepest needs of the heart, which are nothing to do with homosexuality or heterosexuality in themselves. So we must recognise that when we are seeking to grow in holiness, our deepest needs can be met by Christ alone.

Godly Same Sex Relationships

So, what do we say then about godly same sex relationships? We should be blessed by these friendships and receive them from God because they are a necessary part of life. They are important in childhood, in adolescence, and in adulthood. Every man in the church needs a least one good male friend who will tell him things as they really are and who will sometimes confront him about his lifestyle. Every woman needs that kind of friendship and intimacy as well. But make sure that these relationships are serving God's purposes and are not selfish or self-serving.

In a later chapter I will look at "Honouring God's Gift of Singleness", but here I would like to say to single people, learn to receive your satisfaction from the *charism* – the gift of singleness that God has for you at this time. If you're praying that it might be a temporary gift, then may God answer your prayers. But singleness *is* a gift from God. It is possible to be so taken up with Him and have Christ's ministry so much on your heart, that you are able to live a fully fulfilled single life, until God calls you into marriage.

God's Plan for Same Sex Relationships

In summary then, we have seen that God's plan for same sex relationships includes the following components:

- Friendship
- Encouragement
- Accountability

- Mentoring
- Partnership in the gospel

Friendship in same sex relationships is so important. Can you imagine how much easier David's struggles were made, knowing that he had a friend who really understood him and was prepared to encourage him? Accountability and mentoring are vital too, because everyone needs someone of the same sex who is prepared to talk straight with them about the issues of life in a way that someone of the opposite sex never can. If I was speaking to a group of men about this topic of sexuality, then my language would be much straighter and down to earth than if I was speaking to a mixed audience, or a female only audience. Finally, building relationships that partner together in the gospel to fulfil God's purposes is the highest blessing of all in same sex relationships.

I've tried to show you that there are two extreme views on same sex relationships: a judgmental view on one hand and a liberal view on the other. Both attitudes are wrong and unhelpful. Judgmental attitudes are harmful because they're just not like Jesus. Jesus welcomed sinners; He loved them and spent time with them; put His arms around them; ate with them; associated with them and loved them right into the kingdom of God. Judgmental attitudes cause rejection and build prejudice, and they arise out of a self-righteousness that proclaims, "We're better than they are, that's why we judge them."

Liberal attitudes are also harmful because they say, "Anything goes, do what you want to do, it doesn't really matter." But such an attitude never faces the reality of the pain and suffering that comes from rejecting God's way. At best, liberal attitudes are a compromise. They bow to political correctness and obscure the harm that sin causes.

God's rules for same sex relationships were established by Him to protect us from damaging ourselves. They are not rules invented by a killjoy God, but safe boundaries born out of the love and compassion of a Father for His children.

Chapter Summary

- The Bible strictly prohibits acts of a sexual nature between members of the same sex, and also between members of the opposite sex outside of marriage.
- The biblical mandate for the use of sexuality cannot be dismissed as relating to ancient cultural or religious practices that are no longer relevant to us. Sexuality is a moral issue and Paul's teaching in Romans shows that deviations from God's standards are unacceptable.
- The issue of gender orientation is currently being widely debated. Are people born gay or do they choose to be gay? There is insufficient scientific evidence to suggest that people are born gay, but there may be highly complex factors leading to a person making that choice.
- Believers today need to reach out with love, humility and compassion to all who are struggling, and offer help. Jesus can break the power of every sin.
- Some people claim to have been "shaped" by various factors leading to their present sexual orientation, but we need to understand that: (1) you are not defined by your sexual orientation; (2) you do have to resist temptation and not give in to it; (3) we all need to deal with issues at a root level, not just at a behavioural level.
- God's rules for same sex relationships were established by Him to protect us from damaging ourselves, born out of God's compassion for us, His children.

HONOURING GOD'S GIFT OF SINGLENESS

One charismatic gift that is not often talked about and still less sought after today, is the gift of singleness. Yet it is a precious gift from God which is given to some, for whom singleness and celibacy is a life calling. When we talk about the charismatic gifts, most of us think of tongues or miracles, but singleness is a gift of the Spirit too – it's not a curse!

Clearly there are certain individuals that God calls to a life of singleness in order to fulfil a specific purpose which He has for them. Such individuals can readily respond to that call and God blesses them with the gift of singleness and celibacy. For most people, marriage will be the norm, but all of us, at one time or another will live single lives. It may be for a short period only, or it may be for a long time, but during that season we too will need the supernatural gift of singleness from God to go forward.

This means that all of us while we are single, can learn to draw on the power of God's gift, even if we are not called to be single for lifelong service. We need to redeem our single years and not despise them as a period of unfruitfulness whilst we are "waiting to get married".

Very often in our culture, singleness is looked down upon. Because of pressures generated by society and even the church, single people can find themselves spending all their time wishing they weren't single; thinking that singleness is "bad"; that there is no value in it; and that it is something that has to be tolerated until they find a partner. That is the wrong way to view your singleness, whether it turns out to be temporary or permanent – not least because there are special blessings that God gives to the single person that aren't available when you are married.

Jesus made an interesting observation about singleness in a conversation with His disciples. The disciples were responding to Jesus after He had spoken about the binding nature of marriage. Jesus said that divorce was not a part of God's plan for His people; it must not happen. Since He taught that marriage was so sacred and binding, the disciples responded:

> *"If such is the case of the man with his wife, it is better not to marry."*
>
> (MATTHEW 19:10)

But Jesus corrected His disciples and in doing so spoke of the fact that there is a special call to a life of celibacy. He said to them:

> *"All cannot accept this saying, but only those to whom it has been given: For there are eunuchs who were born thus from their mother's womb, and there are eunuchs who were made eunuchs by men, and there are eunuchs who have made themselves eunuchs for the kingdom of heaven's sake. He who is able to accept it, let him accept it."*
>
> (MATTHEW 19:11–12)

Jesus explained that there were three types of "eunuchs" – i.e. those who would never marry. The first category of person included those who were born physically incapable of having relations with a woman, and who therefore would not marry in Jesus' culture. The second category of person included those who were "made eunuchs by men" as Jesus put it. In many of the palaces of the ancient world the servants would be eunuchs – especially those who served in the wives' quarters, because they could be trusted. This is where the name originated, "eunuch" being formed from the Greek words *eune* meaning "bed" and *ekhein* meaning "to keep" – literally "bed-keeper".

But Jesus says that there is a third type of "eunuch" – those who make themselves eunuchs for the sake of the kingdom of heaven. Of course, this doesn't mean that these people have had themselves castrated in order to make themselves *physical* eunuchs. Rather, Jesus is saying there are those who, for the greater service of the kingdom of God, have sought and received the gift of celibacy in order to be more effective in, and dedicated to, the task God has given them.

It is important to note here that Jesus does not say that celibacy is the norm. The Bible teaches that marriage is God's will generally for everyone. We see that from the very beginning of mankind's existence God commands Adam and Eve to be fruitful and to fill the earth. However, Jesus says that singleness and celibacy is a special gift for those *"... to whom it has been given"* (Matthew 19:11). Not everyone can accept this, Jesus says, but those who have this call on their lives can accept it and should accept it.

One thing that I want to make clear is this: people who are called to lifelong celibacy will know about it. If that is you, God will have called you to it, and you will have responded. If you are a person who really wants to be married, then don't think that God is going to call you to live out your worst nightmare – a life of singleness. The Bible says that, *"He who finds a wife finds a good thing"* (Proverbs 18:22). If your heart's desire is to be married, then God won't call you to a life of singleness. But people who are specifically called to receive the gift of singleness will find total fulfilment in the kingdom of God and their relationship with Jesus.

One of the fallacies heard so often today, which I touched upon in a previous chapter, is that single people will not be emotionally fulfilled or satisfied until they are married. That simply is not the case. There are benefits to marriage that you don't get in singleness, but equally there are benefits to singleness that you don't get in marriage. Getting married does not equal emotional fulfilment and completion – it does not work like that. If you are not fulfilled in your singleness, then you never will be in your married life. It is only Jesus who can give you complete emotional fulfilment.

The Call to Singleness

The call to singleness and celibacy has been honoured by many Church traditions. In Roman Catholicism for instance, the call to celibacy still exists for priests, and for nuns entering strictly controlled religious communities. Such institutions interpret the Bible as saying that in order to be set apart for special service to God, they must be single and celibate. As evangelicals, we have not historically recognised the need for singleness and ministry calling to be so closely connected. Along with many other evangelical Christians, you might think to insist a priest remains unmarried puts an unnecessary burden on them.

Most monastic traditions call for singleness/celibacy as a prerequisite. Whilst there are sincere and noble reasons for this, I believe it can force celibacy on those who, whilst they are called to be set apart for God, are not called to be single/celibate. This is why many members of religious groups become susceptible to committing sexual sins. They are suppressing their natural sexual drives which should be directed towards mutual fulfilment in the context of marriage, and have not specifically received the supernatural gift of singleness.

The Roman Catholic Church in particular has gone through very troubled times with accusations of sexual abuse being levelled at many of its priests. One reason for this problem is surely that there are priests functioning within the church who don't want to be single or celibate and who are therefore struggling with issues that God never intended them to struggle with.

Historically, there have also been groups within Protestant Christianity who have highly valued celibacy, but with a different emphasis. Often these believers have "exaggerated" the call to singleness/celibacy as though it is superior to marriage and is somehow essential for those who are striving to attain a "higher level" of holiness. When I was a young believer, I recall one lady in my church whose attitude to marriage was that it was for those who weren't "spiritual enough" to stay single!

She was one of a number of believers who took Paul's teaching literally when he said, *"It is better to marry than to burn with passion"* (1 Corinthians 7:9), thinking that it refers to people who cannot control their lust and therefore must get married. Later on in this chapter we will look at that verse in context and find out why that was *not* what Paul was teaching.

Marriage Is the Normal Pursuit for Most People

The Bible clearly teaches that marriage is good, honourable and the norm for most people. Hebrew 13:4 says:

> *"Marriage is honourable among all, and the bed undefiled; but fornicators and adulterers God will judge."*

Marriage was designed by God and given in the creation mandate as part of our service to Him. Marriage, this verse in Hebrews teaches us, is actually an *aid* to holiness, rather than a way out for those who aren't holy enough. And in Ephesians 5:25–27 Paul shows that there is a "cleansing" aspect to the marriage relationship that has a parallel in Christ's cleansing of His Bride – the Church.

God's plan for marriage is that the husband will bring his wife into a closer relationship with God and vice versa. Singleness is not a vehicle through which a person is called into a deeper intimacy with God than marriage allows – it is a gift from God, different from marriage, that is equally fulfilling in its own way. Neither marriage nor singleness is a superior calling.

Some people cite Paul's teaching in 1 Corinthians 7 as the basis for claiming that singleness is more "spiritual" than marriage. It is worth looking closely at these verses, because a superficial reading could give the impression that Paul was commending a life of celibacy over marriage. 1 Corinthians 7:1–2 says:

> *"Now concerning the things of which you wrote to me: It is good for a man not to touch a woman. Nevertheless, because of sexual immorality, let each man have his own wife, and let each woman have her own husband."*

And in 1 Corinthians 6–7 Paul writes,

> *"But I say this as a concession, not as a commandment. For I wish that all men were even as I myself. But each one has his own gift from God, one in this manner and another in that."*

In these verses Paul seems to be suggesting that he would prefer everyone to remain single. At that time Paul himself was not married, although it is likely that he was married at some point, as most men in the Pharisaic order were. It may be that he was a widower, and then remained celibate, having been blessed by God with the gift of singleness. Paul does say he wishes everyone were single like him so that they could be equally devoted to the cause of the gospel, but he qualifies his remark by following it with, *"But each one has his own gift from God."* Marriage is a gift from God, as is singleness.

Then in 1 Corinthians 7:8–9 Paul says:

> *"But I say to the unmarried and to the widows: It is good for them if they remain even as I am; but if they cannot exercise self-control, let them marry. For it is better to marry than to burn with passion."*

And later in 1 Corinthians 7:32–34 he expands his thoughts on singleness versus marriage in the context of serving God:

> *"But I want you to be without care. He who is unmarried cares for the things of the Lord – how he may please the Lord. But he who is married cares about the things of the world – how he may please his wife. There is a difference between a wife and a virgin. The unmarried woman cares about the things of the Lord, that she may be holy both in body and in spirit. But she who is married cares about the things of the world – how she may please her husband."*

Having read those passages it does sound as though Paul is saying it is better to be single than to be married – that if you can't live a super-holy life by remaining single, then it's better for you to deal with your lustful desires by getting married. But we need to understand Paul's words in context. Is Paul saying here that the precious gift of marriage, given and commended by God in Genesis, and confirmed by Jesus as the will of God, is actually the least preferred option because it interferes with your relationship with Him? No. Paul is not contradicting the clear teaching found elsewhere in Scripture. He is addressing a particular situation in Corinth that the Christians there had asked about. 1 Corinthians 7:26 is the key to understanding these phrases:

> *"I suppose therefore that this is good* ***because of the present distress*** *– that it is good for a man to remain as he is."*
>
> (emphasis added)

Paul makes it clear that it is because of a current crisis in the church, which he describes as *"the present distress"*, that he is saying these things. We are not told specifically what the distress is that the Corinthian Christians are experiencing – it could have been persecution, or problems with their pagan neighbours, or perhaps Christians marrying non-Christians. We simply don't know, but it is clear that Paul is not making a rule that applies to all people, everywhere, at all times. He is making a rule that applies to the present circumstances for that group of believers in order to address a particular need.

When Paul spoke of remaining single so as not to be "distracted" (verse 35), and to be thoroughly focused on the things of God, it could well be that he did so because the Corinthians were facing persecution – and in a time of persecution and pressure, our attention needs to be completely directed towards God. It's easy to understand, for example, how in situations of persecution, where Christians are being killed for their faith, that it would be better not to marry under those extreme conditions. A time of warfare is not a good time to think about getting married. But even then, Paul makes it clear that if people do marry under these conditions, then they have not sinned (see 1 Corinthians 7:2, 9, 25, 35).

What About Christians Today?

Paul's words in 1 Corinthians 7 have a lot to teach us as modern believers, whether we remain single or get married. There are three things that I particularly want to highlight in summary:

1. ***It is God who gives the gift of singleness to some and not others***. In 1 Corinthians 7:7 Paul says, *"Each one has his own gift from God."* The word translated gift is *charism* which is the word to describe a grace gift from God – a special dispensation given to a person by Him. In the case of singleness it is given to some, but not to others. Marriage is God's norm for most people.
2. ***Everyone should seek God before they marry***. It is sensible for every person to ask the Lord, "Are you calling me to remain single?" before embarking on something as serious as marriage. Usually, the answer will be "No." Those who have been specially called to remain single will usually have realised it long before marriage is an issue, as the Holy Spirit will have spoken into their heart.

3. ***We all need the gift of singleness until we are married.*** Singleness is a grace gift from God and we all need this grace as long as we are single. It is perhaps easier for people to see marriage as a "supernatural" gift from God, but singleness is equally supernatural in nature when imparted to us by God.

As a pastor and a counsellor, I am frequently asked by single people, "What do I do? I'm created as a sexual person – that's part of who I am – and I'm not married at the moment. The Bible teaches that sexuality should only be expressed within the confines of marriage, but how do I deal with my sexual urges?"

One thing I can say in response to that is, "There is an anointing available for you in the gift of singleness that you can walk in." This is not cop-out statement – it's true! The gift of singleness is truly a supernatural blessing from God that can enable you to be completely fulfilled during that season. God can and will give you the strength to control your sexual urges and live in peace, not turmoil and frustration, until your season of singleness comes to an end.

Using the Season of Singleness Positively

Some people are so obsessed with the idea that they must be married – and soon – that they miss out on the fun and blessing of being single. God wants us to enjoy every season of our lives – both singleness and marriage – and we should not be in such a hurry to dismiss that which God has ordained for our blessing.

As a result of constantly longing for a partner, some don't appreciate their singleness until they look back on it from the perspective of marriage. Guys, remember those days when you could tune in to Sky Sports every night and watch football whenever you wanted? Now you are married you have to flip over to Sky Movies and watch some romantic film like *Notting Hill* – and not only that, you have to watch it knowing that your favourite team are on the other channel!

There are plenty of things you can do when you're single that you can't do when you are married. When you are married you don't have quite the same freedom to travel wherever you want to or to do whatever you want whenever you feel like it. Of course, such things are more than compensated for by the blessings of marriage, but the point is: make the most your singleness while you can, and then make the most of your marriage.

Learn to use you single years positively. Don't just drift through life thinking that all the fun, enjoyment and satisfaction is going to start from the moment you walk down the aisle. There is a freedom you have as a single person that can be used for a positive purpose as Paul notes in 1 Corinthians 7:32 when he says, *"I want you to be without care. He who is unmarried cares for the things of the Lord – how he may please the Lord."* When you are single there are things that you can do for God that simply would not be practical if you were married. You are available to be used by God in ways that married couples are not. Again, that does not mean that the value of marriage is diminished in any way – it simply means: "Use your singleness wisely."

If you are a single person who longs to be married, then

ask God to grant you that desire of your heart according to His timing for your life. To desire to be married is a good desire to have. Enjoy your wedding, enjoy your marriage and all of its benefits; but while you are single, enjoy that and know that you are anointed for it for a time. Although there are pressures that you face as a single person, there are different pressures you will face as a married person.

Whether you are single for the long haul or whether you are single for a temporary period, you still need God's gift of His Spirit and there is purpose in your singleness. That's why I called this chapter "*Honouring* God's Gift of Singleness" – because God calls the gift of marriage precious and He also calls the gift of singleness precious. Both are to be honoured and cherished in their season.

Chapter Summary

- The gift of singleness is a charismatic gift that is not often talked about.
- There are certain individuals for whom singleness and celibacy is a life calling, but everyone will be single at some point in their life. Whether we are single for a long or a short period of time, we all need to draw on the power of God's gift.
- Jesus identified that there exists a special calling of celibacy some people are able to accept in order to more effective in, or dedicated to, the task God has given them.
- Jesus did not teach that celibacy should be the norm. The Bible is clear that marriage is the normal pursuit for most people.
- The apostle Paul seemed to suggest that singleness was preferable, but his comments were made in the context of a crisis in the Corinthian church. He was not setting a standard for all Christians of all times.
- Whether we remain single or married, Paul highlights three important principles for us: (1) it is God who gives the gift of singleness to some and not to others; (2) everyone should seek God before they marry; (3) we all need the gift of singleness until we are married.
- We should use our season of singleness positively and not be hasty to dismiss that which God has ordained for our blessing.

CHAPTER 8

FREEDOM FROM SOUL TIES

by Amanda Dye

We have seen that sex is a precious gift that God gives us as an expression of love and intimacy in marriage. We have also learnt that Satan will try to take this gift and pervert it in any way he can – to distort it into something that God never intended. No discussion on modern sexuality would be complete then, without examining the area of "soul ties" – a topic that has sometimes been viewed as mysterious or controversial – but one that demands our attention, since Satan has spread the lie that it is OK to have many sexual partners in life.

In this chapter we will look at the emotional damage that is caused when a person pursues many sexual relationships. Such promiscuity results in a bondage being created in that person's life, known as a soul tie. Later we will also look at how to break free from such bondage and receive healing, but for now we will begin by defining soul ties. A soul tie is simply this: an emotional or mental attachment that brings a person into bondage.

In essence, sexual sin is an *attitude*. In an earlier chapter, I defined sexual sin as "any attitude, thought or action that is not directed towards the fulfilment of your partner in marriage". If sexual purity is the opposite of sexual sin, then it is a high ideal; one that many people – both unbelievers and believers – fall short of. Many single Christians, for instance, find it a huge struggle to keep themselves pure until marriage. Thankfully, there is forgiveness and deliverance in Jesus' name for anyone who falls, whether in their thought life, or physically. God is a loving Father and He forgives our sins when we genuinely repent. It is possible therefore, to win the struggle with sexual sin and learn to use God's gift of sex in a way that honours Him.

Men and women have to battle against the temptation of sexual sin in different ways, simply because we are made differently. In her book, *Every Woman's Battle*, Shannon Eldridge writes:

> "Men and women struggle in different ways when it comes to sexual integrity. While a man's battle begins with what he takes in through his eyes, a woman's begins in the heart and her thoughts. A man must guard his eyes to maintain sexual integrity but because God made woman to be emotionally and mentally stimulated, we women must closely guard our hearts and minds as well as our bodies if we want to experience God's plan for sexual and emotional fulfilment. A woman's battle is for sexual and emotional integrity."[1]

For some men and women however, the battle against sexual sin seems to be unrelenting. After confessing and repenting of their sin numerous times, they still fall back into well-worn patterns. They continue to struggle with the same issues, but they never really understand why. Most likely they will be living for God, reading their Bibles, praying every day and seeking to move on with God, and at the same time struggling to control their sexual urges and to bringing their thoughts in line with God's Word.

These same people may be unnaturally drawn back into their former lifestyles – much as they don't want to be. They find themselves constantly pulled back and they cannot find freedom from former sexual and emotional relationships. Why is that? The answer to both the problem of repetitive sin and the constant pull of the past usually involves unhealthy soul ties. They are very powerful, deep-rooted bonds that need to be broken before complete freedom will come.

Three Types of Bondage

There are basically three types of bondage that can become established in a person's life. Bondage can be *physical*, such as dependency addictions to drugs or alcohol. Bondage can be *mental or emotional*, such as soul ties; and bondage can be *spiritual*, originating from demonic influence. Each type of bondage will set you on a course of self-destruction if it is not dealt with. We need to understand all three dimensions in order to deal effectively with compulsive behaviour, but often the dimension that escapes our notice is the soul tie resulting in emotional bondage.

In drug addiction, the physical dependence on the drug can be dealt with and "cured" in a matter of days through medical treatment and detoxification. But the emotional/psychological dependence on the drug takes much, much longer to deal with. Emotional bondage is usually the strongest factor affecting a person's behaviour. Just because a person's body is "clean" from drugs, it doesn't mean they are free from their addiction. They won't truly be free until the underlying personal, psychological and emotional problems that caused them to begin taking drugs are dealt with. Those problems remain and invariably have to be worked out through a process of counselling.

Similarly, the spiritual or demonic element often associated with addictive/compulsive behaviour is usually quite easy to deal with. Deliverance can happen in a moment in the name of Jesus and He has given us all authority and power to cast out demons and deal with demonic influences of every kind. But often the underlying emotional issues in a person's life can take longer to work out so that they are totally free.

Sex Is Not Just a Physical Act

To understand the damaging potential of soul ties, one has to understand that sex is not merely a physical act, but a spiritual one also. Mostly people when they talk about "having sex", certainly those outside of Christ, are referring only to the physical act. But it is much more than that. The Bible says when two join together in sexual union they become "one flesh" or "one person" (Genesis 2:24). In sex, there is not just a physical union, but a union of soul and spirit.

The Bible teaches that every person is made up of body, soul and spirit. These three components make up our whole being and we cannot separate what we do with our bodies from the rest of our being. If you enter into a sexual relationship with a person who is not your husband/wife, then you connect with them on a soul/spirit level, not just with your body. That is what makes sexual sin so appalling in the sight of the Lord – especially for a believer. The apostle Paul likened it to taking the Lord and joining Him with the person you unite to in the act of sexual sin! In 1 Corinthians 6:15–17 we read:

> *"Do you not know that your bodies are members of Christ? Shall I then take the members of Christ and make them members of a harlot? Certainly not! Or do you not know that he who is joined to a harlot is one body with her? For 'the two,' He says, 'shall become one flesh.' But he who is joined to the Lord is one spirit with Him."*

This is an incredibly powerful and sobering scripture. Paul is saying that for a Christian to enter into a sexual relationship with someone other than their husband/wife is like taking Jesus' body to be joined with a harlot. As a Christian, our bodies are temples in which God dwells. Christ lives in us by His Spirit and our bodies belong to God, to be set apart and sanctified for service to Him. It is a dreadful thought that we would defile the place where God lives through an illicit sexual union.

Not only does sexual sin defile your own body, it defiles the other person as well. Since you become "joined" spiritually and emotionally to any person you have sex with, if this is not your husband/wife i.e. if it's a sinful union, then it gives Satan an opportunity to cause spiritual and emotional bondage to "pass" between the two people. That's why sexual sin can result in such deep bondage. We are not only defiling our own body, but we are opening ourselves up to the possibility of becoming entangled in the sin and spiritual problems of the person we are having sex with.

In spiritual terms, the only "safe sex" you can ever have is with your marriage partner. If you're involved in a sinful sexual relationship, then you're having "unprotected sex". Safe sex is sex in accordance with God's will and purpose. Everybody knows about sexually transmitted diseases, but what about sexually transmitted bondages or curses? Condoms may give you some measure of protection against physical diseases, but they cannot protect you from the bondages and curses that come from sin.

Shannon Eldridge says:

> "The only way to help protect yourself is to guard against sexual compromise altogether. No condom fully protects you against the physical consequences of

sexual, immoral behaviour. Even more important, no condom protects you against the spiritual consequences of sin, broken fellowship with God. No condom will protect you from the emotional consequences of a broken heart, therefore don't think in terms of safe sex but in terms of saving sex until marriage."[2]

The Nature of Soul Ties

1. They come through sexual sin or emotional ties bordering on sexual sin

We have seen that soul ties are established through the physical aspect of sexual sin, but soul ties can also come about through unhealthy emotional ties which are *bordering* on sexual sin. Remember that sexual sin affects the body, soul and spirit, operating on an emotional as well as a physical level. What you do with your mind can be almost as damaging as what you do with your body, and the Bible teaches that "mental" immorality and adultery are as serious as their physical counterparts.

Jesus said in Matthew 5:28,

> *"But I say to you that whoever looks at a woman* [or man] *to lust for her* [or him] *has already committed adultery with her* [or him] *in his* [or her] *heart."*

Jesus clearly is teaching that if we look at someone lustfully we are committing sin in our heart, just as much as if we were physically committing adultery with them. This is perhaps the most difficult kind of sin to deal with, mainly because it is the sort of sin that no one except you and God know you've committed. Nevertheless, it is a sin that must be dealt with as ruthlessly as any other. If you are persistently giving in to lustful thoughts that are directed towards another person, then you are establishing an unhealthy emotional soul tie that will be a destructive force in your life.

2. Soul ties bind you to former patterns of thought and behaviour

People who were sexually promiscuous in the past will often find it very hard to give up their former patterns of thought and behaviour, even though they desire to put those things behind them and move on. This is because their emotional life is *fragmented* due to soul ties.

I heard about the case of one young Christian couple who were boyfriend and girlfriend and had a close, intense relationship. In due course their relationship ended and they both married other people. But try as he might, the man just could not put his former girlfriend out of his mind. He talked about her frequently; he often compared his wife with her, and emotionally he kept the relationship with her "alive". He had not actually had sex with his former girlfriend, but had formed a very deep emotional bond with her that he did not address before getting married. As a result, today his marriage is over. This young man could not escape his former thinking and behavioural patterns due to the unresolved soul tie with this girl.

3. Soul ties can be the reason for further sexual sin and bondage

Soul ties are sometimes the real cause behind a pattern of behaviour that leads a person into sin. In other words, it's not that you deliberately go out to commit sin, but because of a soul tie from a former relationship, you keep being drawn back into your old life and tempted to sin as you did previously. We are all responsible for our own actions, and no excuse allows us to abdicate our responsibility for our sin, but it can be an unresolved soul tie that brings us to the edge of temptation and draws us into sin time and again.

Again, from *Every Woman's Battle*, listen to the testimony of one woman trapped in sexual sin. She says:

> "I was seeking to understand why I still felt tempted outside my marriage so my counsellor asked me to spend a week making a list of every man I'd ever been with sexually or had pursued emotionally. I was shocked and saddened to see how long my list had grown through the years. At the next visit she asked me to spend a week praying and asking myself, 'What do each of these men have in common?' God showed me that each relationship had been with someone who was older than I and in some form of authority over me – my professor, my boss, my lawyer. As I searched my soul to discern why such a common thread existed in my relationship pursuits, the root of the issue became evident: my hunger for power over a man."[3]

This story illustrates aptly the stumbling block that unresolved soul ties present to future freedom and purity.

4. Soul ties are often linked to unforgiveness

Soul ties are usually connected to the issue of unforgiveness. Inevitably, when deep and intense relationships break apart, hurt and bitterness are left in their wake, and this will often lead to unforgiveness. But we can never be free until we release forgiveness to others, no matter how much they may have wounded us. Forgiveness is a vital key to finding freedom from emotional and sexual bondage. In Luke 6:37–38 we read:

> *"Judge not, and you shall not be judged. Condemn not, and you shall not be condemned. Forgive, and you will be forgiven. Give, and it will be given to you: good measure, pressed down, shaken together, and running over will be put into your bosom. For with the same measure that you use, it will be measured back to you."*

Preachers very often use this verse when taking up offerings, but it has a much wider meaning. What you sow, you will reap. If you sow unforgiveness, then you will reap bitterness. But if you sow forgiveness, then you will reap grace and mercy from God.

The measure that you use for others will be the standard by which it will be measured back to you. If you hold on to unforgiveness, then you will never be free of that thing you are refusing to forgive – and you will be suffering untold emotional and spiritual damage.

Ephesians 4:26–27 says:

> *" 'Be angry, and do not sin': do not let the sun go down on your wrath, nor give place to the devil."*

We need to make absolutely sure that we are not harbouring bitterness or unforgiveness towards anyone who has hurt us in the past, because, as this verse teaches, such grievances give the devil access to our lives.

Freedom from Soul Ties

In summary, I want to leave with you seven steps you can follow in order to break the power of ungodly soul ties and begin to walk in freedom:

1. Confess the sinful contact you have had, whether it is emotional or actually involved the sexual act. The first question to ask yourself is, "Do I want to be free from this?" If the answer is yes, then you must begin to do business with God.
2. Renounce the ungodly relationship, naming the person or the situation. Since sin is specific, repentance must be too. Identifying the person or situation before God ensures that you are on the same wavelength.
3. Forsake the ungodly relationship utterly before God, from your heart. Repentance is a change of heart and must be sincere and honest before God.
4. Forgive everyone who has offended or used and abused you in the past. Identify each person and then release forgiveness to that individual.
5. Break all contact with the person [in the case of former sexual partners], including disposing of any tokens, keepsakes, gifts, photos, or anything belonging to that individual/relationship. Get rid of them, because as long as you are holding on to them, you are holding on to that relationship and the memory of that person.

6. Receive prayer for deliverance from your church elders or ministry team. Soul ties need prayer for deliverance in a similar way to demonic bondages.
7. Turn your heart to God for all your needs. Once your sin has been dealt with and the bondage of the past broken, resolve in your heart never to revisit it, and depend on God for the strength and grace to go forward.

If these seven steps are followed faithfully, then they will result in freedom from soul ties and the ability to move forward in God unhindered by the past.

Chapter Summary

- When a person pursues many sexual relationships, emotional damage is caused. Promiscuity results in a bondage being created which is known as a "soul tie".
- If a person's battle against sexual sin seems to be unrelenting, and they are constantly drawn back into former patterns of behaviour, then the probable cause is soul ties. They are deep-rooted bonds that need to be broken before complete freedom will come.
- Soul ties are a form of mental and emotional bondage. Whereas physical bondage can be treated and "cured" relatively quickly, emotional bondage usually needs to be dealt with through counselling over time.
- Sex is not just a physical act, but a spiritual one that involves a union of soul and spirit between two people. The more sexual relationships a person engages in, the more "fragmented" their soul/emotions become.
- Sexual sin defiles not only your own body, but the other person's body as well. It opens the way for other sexual/emotional bondages to "pass" between the parties involved. The only "safe sex" you can ever have is with your marriage partner.
- There are four key aspects about the nature of soul ties: (1) they come from sexual sin or emotional ties bordering on sin; (2) soul ties bind you to former patterns of thought or behaviour; (3) soul ties can be the reason for further sexual sin and bondage; (4) soul ties are often linked to unforgiveness.
- There are seven steps that you can follow to find freedom from soul ties as listed above.

What Needs Sex Does Not Fill

The Problem of Lust

The act of sex fulfils a basic, physical need of all human beings. The sexual drive is given to us by God so that we will desire it to be satisfied – and the way to that satisfaction is through the mutual enjoyment of intimate sexual relations within marriage. Sexual intimacy within marriage fulfils our needs perfectly, but if we simply pursue the fulfilment of those desires in any way that seems best to us – i.e. outside of marriage – then, sooner or later, we will find we are satisfying no need at all. A legitimate desire given to us by God will have been turned into lust, and the thing about lust is that it is never satisfied! Sex outside of marriage will ultimately be a very unfulfilling and hollow experience. It is not a true expression of love, because love desires to give and not to get.

The apostle Paul makes it clear that each of us is called to live a clean and holy life and reveals the devastating effects of lust. His reference is to the whole of life generally, but he includes sex in his remarks. He begins by saying:

> *"This I say, therefore, and testify in the Lord, that you should no longer walk as the rest of the Gentiles walk, in the futility of their mind . . ."*
>
> (Ephesians 4:17)

Paul refers to "futile" or "pointless" thinking. The pursuit of pleasure and lust outside of God's purposes is pointless. He continues in the next verse:

> *". . . having their understanding darkened, being alienated from the life of God, because of the ignorance that is in them, because of the blindness of their heart."*
>
> (Ephesians 4:18)

Paul then tells us what spiritual blindness and ignorance lead to, and how the Christian should deal with issues of their "former conduct".

> *"… who, being past feeling, have given themselves over to lewdness, to work all uncleanness with greediness. But you have not so learned Christ, if indeed you have heard Him and have been taught by Him, as the truth is in Jesus: that you put off, concerning your former conduct, the old man which grows corrupt according to the deceitful lusts, and be renewed in the spirit of your mind, and that you put on the new man which was created according to God, in true righteousness and holiness."*
>
> (Ephesians 4:19–24)

What Paul is teaching is that the lust that drives people to seek satisfaction produces only more lust – in fact, an insatiable desire for more. This is why it is a fallacy to believe that if you have sex with someone you are solving a problem for yourself: the need to satisfy your sexual drive. Illicit sex may give a momentary thrill and a fleeting sense of satisfaction, but ultimately you are just feeding a lust that will never be satisfied. The only way to deal with lust is to starve it to death! Give it nothing to eat.

Men and women are wired differently when it comes to sexual matters and each needs to guard their sexual integrity in different ways. Men are stimulated most by what they see, so for men it means "bouncing" your eyes and not letting them rest where they should not be resting. For women, it is more important that your emotions are guarded than your eyes. God's gift of sex is a means of expressing love in marriage, but it can never be a substitute for love, or a means of obtaining it. Over the years Amanda and I have counselled many ladies who have fallen into sexual sin because they thought they could use their body to buy the love of a man. It is simply not true.

Differences Between the Sexes

I'm sure you didn't need to pick this book up in order to learn that men and women are different! Nevertheless, a biblical examination of those differences is valuable, because so often we overlook them or find them to be stumbling blocks to maintaining successful relationships.

One of the most wonderful aspects of God's diverse creation is that He created a number of differences between the sexes, yet we are one humanity. In Genesis 1:27–28 we read:

> *"So God created man in His own image; in the image of God He created him; male and female He created them. Then God blessed them, and God said to them, 'Be fruitful and multiply; fill the earth and subdue it; have dominion over the fish of the sea, over the birds of the air, and over every living thing that moves on the earth.' "*

Equal but different

Notice that when God created man (as it's translated in the NKJV), He created man male and female. A better translation might be, "So God created humanity" or "human beings" because the word "man" in this verse doesn't mean male as opposed to female; it means "human". God created "people", made in His own image, male and female, and these two are *equal* but *different.*

Equal in dignity and worth

Men and women are totally equal in their dignity and worth. Both were made in the image of God. Some Bible scholars used to teach that it was the man who *carried* the image of God. I want to suggest that no greater liberation has ever come to the female species on this earth than through the Word of God, which reveals the true equality of men and women!

The truth is that all of us, men and women alike, bear the image of God, and what is important is that each of us reflects that image. As distinct yet complementary sexes, we are ultimately to reflect the heart and purpose of God within the covenant of marriage. The only exception are those to whom God has given the gift of singleness – a unique gift of God that blesses an individual with an extraordinary ability to reflect the glory of God and the completion of God as a single person. It's beautiful when it happens and it's tragic when people miss it.

Equal in call and commission

Men and women were also created equal in call and commission. Both have been called to be fruitful and have dominion in the earth, especially together in partnership. God's command was, *"Be fruitful and multiply."* Try and do that on your own if you're a man!

Different in gender and role

So men and women are equal in their standing before God, but different in their gender. The first difference that is obvious about gender is that men and women have distinct anatomical and physiological differences. God designed the bodies of men and women to be compatible. It is obvious that sexual intercourse between a man and a woman is a natural joining together of two complementary bodies; and that sex between two men or two women is therefore unnatural. While members of the same sex can engage in sexual activity, surely no-one would argue that homosexual activity is anatomically or physiologically compatible.

The fact that God designed sexual intercourse to function as it does, is, I believe an amazing picture of the call upon the lives of men and women. God designed sex so that the male must penetrate the female. It is a picture of the male and female roles in life: the man has been called to lead and take initiative and the woman has been called to be a receptive helper.

Sex goes far beyond a mere function designed to perpetuate the human race, enticing us to continue reproducing. God has blessed us as men and women to be equal, but to have different roles – different roles in producing children; different roles in life, which are an extension of what we discover about ourselves anatomically and physiologically.

Men and women are also very different emotionally – we have very different needs which need fulfilling and different emotions which need to be expressed. And I believe that there is also a spiritual difference between men and women. Some might find that a controversial statement, but I simply mean that each has a distinct spiritual role and function. Men are called to be loving leaders and women are called to be submissive helpers.

A man's sexual/emotional needs

It is important to understand these basic differences as they pertain to the sexual relationship between a husband and wife, and how each will want to express themselves in that relationship. For instance, for men the physical aspect of sex is very important. It is part of their natural drive as men. In most cases, men are built to be physically stronger than women (though of course, there will always be the exception!) and so it is natural that they will often take a strong, physical initiative in the act of lovemaking.

Men feel an inherent need to be the "stronger sex". Unfortunately, that has been perverted outside of Christ into a sexuality that is often dominant and abusive. I have been shocked when I have entered the locker room of my local gym to hear talk about women that I thought would have been left behind in the playground. If women could hear the way some men talk, then they would never, ever be taken in by the seductive talk of another man again! It's all about showing off and physical conquest. To listen to them you would think they are competing to be champion stallions in a stud farm! But that kind of demeaning attitude towards women, and bragging about physical prowess is not of God. There is much more to being a man; manhood can only be conferred upon you by the quality of your character in life.

A woman's sexual/emotional needs

For women the needs are so different. A woman is looking for security in her relationship; for a sense of value and fulfilment. Their partner has to be someone they can trust, respect and feel safe with.

There is a saying that's often quoted: men give love in order to get sex and women give sex in order to get love. I understand how the originator of that statement arrived at his/her conclusion, but if you take it at face value, it is perhaps one of the most misleading things that you could ever say about sex.

Love cannot be bought, not even with sex, and if men give love in order to get sex then it's actually not love that they're giving. And if women give sex in order to get love then it's not love that they're getting, because everybody knows *you can't buy love.* You can't buy love with your money and you can't buy love with your body. If it can be bought, it's not love; love can only be given, it cannot be taken.

Sex will not buy you anything and sex will not fulfil you in any deeply significant way, physically, emotionally or spiritually. It is a means of expressing love, not getting it. It is a means of fulfilling somebody else rather than being fulfilled yourself. That's why in any relationship, love must always come first. Love must come first, because if sex is an expression of love, *then* it works.

God's Covenant of Love

But even love on its own is not enough. In order for it to be directed in a meaningful way, love must be expressed in a covenant commitment. When God expressed His love for His people, He didn't just leave His love hanging in the air, crying out, "I love you My people!" Instead, He said, "I am committed to you. I will be your God and you will be My people." That is the same basis on which the marriage relationship is founded. It is a covenant commitment of love.

God's covenant name "Yahweh" (see Exodus 3) means "I AM". This is a statement of action not of abstraction. God promises to be whatever we need Him to be. He says, "I will never leave you; I will never forsake you; I am that 'I AM'; I will stand with you; I will rescue you; I will deliver you; I will be your God and you will be My son, My daughter." God expresses His love towards us in a covenant – the characteristic covenant promise expressed in Exodus 6:7:

> *"I will take you as My people, and I will be your God. Then you shall know that I am the LORD your God who brings you out from under the burdens of the Egyptians."*

Marriage is the covenant of love that you make with your husband or wife, for life. When you commit yourselves as husband and wife you are promising to be one another's partner until death; to become one flesh with each other. It is an exclusive, monogamous commitment for *life* between a man and a woman.

Sex is the holy of holies of that relationship. It is an expression of love within that covenant commitment. That's why true love waits. I stress that again and again because so many people think that they need a physical, sexual relationship to fulfil their emotional needs. If you put two people together who are looking to a sexual relationship to fulfil them it is a disaster waiting to happen, because their entire relationship will be driven by a misunderstanding. Sex is a very potent force, but it won't meet your emotional needs.

The Potent Force of Sex

In chapter 1 I mentioned that our church staff once brought in a professional sex therapist to advise us on the issues that her clients commonly raised. We wanted her to open our eyes to the real issues people were discussing "out there" in the world, because as Christians we can sometimes live very sheltered lives. Knowing that we viewed sex as belonging strictly within the confines of marriage, she said to us, "It's all very well for you people to say what you say about sex, but what do you do with the animal inside of you?"

A humanistic worldview

The animal inside of you? Wow! That loaded statement is so revealing about the mindset that most people live with. There are basically two worldviews that prevail in modern society – humanistic versus biblical.

In simple terms, the humanistic worldview sees humans as sophisticated animals having evolved to our present state through natural forces and laws of nature. We are highly evolved, but animals nonetheless. According to this philosophy sex evolved as a means of protecting our genes and ensuring that they survive to the next generation. Sex is governed by the laws of the jungle; it becomes a matter of the fittest, leanest, meanest mating machine impregnating as many as possible to guarantee the survival of its genes. If that is what people are taught to believe, is it any wonder that there is so much sexual chaos in our society? That explains a lot about human sexual behaviour! Even marriage, a social convenience established down the centuries, becomes little more than a vehicle to ensure that my genes survive. That is the "animal" that scientists and humanists say we are.

Despite all of this, what still puzzles me is, how could heterosexual reproduction ever evolve? How did humans come into being before that? It's a question that there is no scientific answer for, which a recent scientific journal admitted, saying "Maybe Darwin got it wrong?" He certainly did. It takes a huge amount of faith to believe that, after a massive cosmic explosion, life was spawned on a lifeless planet and reached the level of complexity and sophistication of modern man. Evolution is not a science, it's a faith!

A biblical worldview

But there is another worldview: that we are not animals, but human beings made in the image of God. In that worldview, sex is a precious gift of a creator God who wills good things for His creation and for humankind made in His image. The pleasure of sex is the gift of love! It is a double gift: given by God for us to enjoy, and for us to bless our partner with in the context of marriage. Our giving of the gift to one another is our expression of love, not a means of gaining anything.

The physical pleasure of sex itself, which has a strong bonding element to it, is a form of superglue that brings two committed people together and binds them so completely that they are one flesh spiritually, mentally, emotionally and even physically. That's the teaching of the Bible. Which "world" would you rather live in?

There are many needs that sex does not fulfil

In summary, I want to highlight again the needs that sex will not fulfil:

- Sex cannot buy you security
- It cannot give you a purpose in life

- It does not make you significant as a person (those who shout the loudest about their exploits are often the most insecure)
- Sex cannot help you make an impact with your life

All these are things that people desire in order to give purpose and meaning to their lives, and so often they think that a great sexual relationship with someone will give them what they want. It is a tragedy, because it never works. The secret of happiness, including sexual happiness, is to find your fulfilment in Christ and to be complete in Him.

Men often look to achieve significance while women often are looking for self-worth. When you know that those needs are met in Christ and in Christ alone, then that which previously drove you from Him into temptation, will now drive you to Him and you will find in Him all the strength that you need to live your life God's way. It will be a joy and a delight.

Once you are full of God and secure in Him, then you are free to love; you are free to give selflessly and unconditionally to another person and you can make a commitment that you will never break. That's what makes love and sex so special.

Chapter Summary

- If we pursue the fulfilment of our sexual desires outside of marriage, then we are turning legitimate desires into lust, and lust can never be satisfied. Paul referred to the devastating effects of lust.
- Men and women are wired differently when it comes to sexual matters. Men are stimulated mostly by what they see and women are stimulated mostly by love and emotional security.
- God created men and women equal but with distinct emotional, physical and spiritual differences.
- Men's emotional needs include expressing themselves physically and asserting their manhood.
- Women's emotional needs include the quest for security, a sense of value, and fulfilment with a partner they can trust and respect.
- Sex is a potent force. A humanistic worldview views sex as an animal instinct that cannot be contained, explaining much about human behaviour in modern society. The biblical worldview views sex as a precious gift of a creator God who wills good things for humankind.
- There are many needs that sex cannot fulfil, including: giving you security, giving you a purpose in life, making you a significant person, helping you make an impact with your life.

APPENDIX

SURVEY OF MEN AND WOMEN'S NEEDS

The teaching contained in this book was brought together as a response to real concerns and questions that individuals in the body of Christ were raising. We asked the members of our congregation to submit anonymously, questions they had regarding sexuality and have endeavoured to answer them as clearly as possible.

We also asked the members to take part in a survey of the emotional needs of both men and women and present the results here as an appendix to the final chapter of the book. We simply asked that each person write down the one thing that they most looked for in the opposite sex. The responses were then gathered into groups and the results can be seen below, ranked in order of popularity.

The results reveal that what a man most wants from a woman is love, support and respect. What a woman most wants from a man is love, communication and friendship.

What Men Want from Women

1. Love

- Love in all its aspects (friendship, romance and sex)
- Someone to be the object of their affection
- Someone who loves them for who they are
- Love, love and more love!

2. Support

- To support even when their career is not going well
- To support their chosen career and to say, "I believe in you."
- To give support, encouragement and affirmation

3. Respect

- Mutual respect and honour
- Respect despite circumstances
- Respect, especially in public

4. Sharing

- Someone to share God's purposes and plans for their life with
- Someone to share interests with
- Someone to share secrets with

5. Communication

- Someone to listen to them
- Someone to understand their needs, concerns and challenges

6. Sex

- Someone to be fulfilled with sexually

7. Submission

- Someone to acknowledge their leadership within the home

8. Companionship

- To be a special friend throughout life's highs and lows
- Someone to feel comfortable with
- Someone to trust

What Women Want from Men

1. Love

- Someone to love them for who they are
- Someone to love and care for them/their children
- Someone who will love, honour and cherish them

2. Communication

- Someone who will listen to them and take them seriously
- Someone to talk to about their feelings
- Someone whom they can talk to about anything
- Someone to talk over issues and problems with

3. Friendship

- Someone who is their best friend
- Someone who is their soulmate
- A friend who will encourage them and help them achieve their potential

4. Honesty/Loyalty/Integrity

- Someone who keeps his word
- Honesty and openness
- Faithfulness
- Someone whom they can trust

5. Romance

- Someone to share romantic times with, not just "quick" sex
- Someone who is romantic or willing to learn how to be

6. Care/Respect/Understanding

- Someone who is caring and considers their needs
- Someone who respects their opinions
- Someone who understands their feelings

7. Help

- Someone who helps them around the home
- Someone who cares for and looks after the children

- Someone who will help to teach the children about God

8. Leadership

- Someone who will lead the family
- Someone who takes the initiative in decision making
- Someone who will set a godly example

Notes

Chapter 1

1. Dr Alex Comfort, *The Joy of Sex*, Pocket Books, 2003.
2. In a later chapter we will discuss the gift of celibacy, which is to be honoured because it is a precious gift that God gives to certain people.
3. NB: It would be advisable for each married couple to look carefully at what method of contraception is appropriate for them, since some modern methods come close to abortion in their method of operation.

Chapter 5

1. The Greek word *eros* doesn't always involve the thought of erotic love and can mean "compassion" or "attraction", but here it is used in the sense of the English word "erotic".

Chapter 6

1. Jeffrey Satinover MD, *Homosexuality and the Politics of Truth*, Baker Books, 1996, p. 129.

Chapter 8

1. Shannon Eldridge, *Every Woman's Battle*, Waterbrook Press, 2003.
2. Ibid.
3. Ibid.

About the Author

Colin Dye is Senior Minister of Kensington Temple and Leader of London City Church, a vibrant and dynamic multicultural church organized into numbers of cells that are active across the city of London. He is an Elim minister and a member of the National Leadership Team of the Elim Pentecostal Churches.

Born in Kenya, East Africa, Colin came to London to train for a profession in the performing arts. Two years later he was arrested by the power of God and became a Christian. In 1975, God took him out of a successful career to attend Romsey House Theological College in Cambridge where he gained a Diploma of Religious Study. This was followed by a BD from London University in 1984.

Since becoming a Christian, Colin's twin desires have been to reach the lost with the gospel and to see revival in the Church. These desires are being realized through his apostolic leadership of Kensington Temple and London City Church, as well as an international ministry stretching from South America through Africa and to the Far East.

Staying Pure in a Sex-Charged World is the twenty-seventh book by Colin whose books have been translated into many European and Asian languages.

Colin is married to Amanda and they have one daughter, Elizabeth.

We hope you enjoyed reading this New Wine book.
For details of other New Wine books
and a range of 2,000 titles from other
Spirit-filled publishers visit our website:
www.newwineministries.co.uk